Memories

by

Patrick J. Lindsay

BLACKWATER PRESS

Printed in Ireland at the press of the publishers 1992
Printed New in Paperback 1993

© Blackwater Press 1993
8, Airton Road,
Tallaght,
Dublin 24.

ISBN: 0 86121 5451

Editor
Brenda McNally

Design & layout
Teresa Burke

Dedication

In memory of Moya and for our children Alison, John and Erris and their children.

Contents

Acknowledgements

This book is called *Memories* because that is what it is. I have never kept a diary or a fee book, so everything which follows is based purely on my recall of events past.

In addition, many of my friends helped make this book possible. Among them are: Dessie and Celine Hynes and their family, whose encouragement, help and hospitality have been immense; James and Heather Morrissey who were of enormous help, especially in the early, bleaker days; Bronwyn Conroy who never failed to prompt me in the right direction; Betty Comerford and Jean Arten who worked wonders with the manuscript, and Jonathan Williams whose editorial advice was very helpful. I must thank too, Murtagh Rabbitte of the well-known tavern and restaurant in Foster Street, Galway, for the facilities he so generously provided to Mike Burns and me at a crucial time. My indebtedness to Maurice Manning and Mike Burns, for their generous and painstaking assistance, can never be repaid. My family have also been extremely supportive – their infinite patience must have been accompanied by great apprehension.

Introduction

Shadows big and small dance slowly on the slopes of the Maamturk Mountains. They dance to the music of the sun. What I propose to write shall not be the music of the sun and the moon and the stars. Rather it shall be the movements prompted by the music of memory, mainly joyful but sometimes sad. And why not? These are the recurring themes of the music of life's journey.

The immediate view of Greatman's Bay, or that part of it north of Bealadangan by the causeway from which access is gained to the island of Annaghvaan, is where I sit intermittently writing, viewing and thinking. Memories flock like the frequent flights of birds. Kilkerrin and Camus Bay begin at the end of the sea view. The land beyond is Rosmuc and further still are the Maamturks. Hidden between are Maamcross, Maam and the great Maam Valley. I think of the lovely Lady Dudley, drowned in Camus on 26 June 1920 having decided to bathe before an attempted reconciliation with her husband.

Rosmuc reminds me of Padraic Pearse and his cottage, but in my view is the Conroy House whence Judge J.C. Conroy came and where the orphaned Sean Phadraic O'Conaire and his brothers Isaac and Michael were reared.

Greatman's Bay is placid now and in it are mirrored the reflections of the mountains whether placid or bounding, with snow-white foaming waves. It is beautiful to behold and one could watch forever the changing colours. It is awesome too, when one thinks of the many lives it has claimed – at least one doctor and several fishermen, rocks and barren little fields are the evidence of a people's life struggle.

1

Annaghvaan is a place of beauty and of peace. The Sabine farm of Horace could be here. Though on mature reflection I don't think it would suit Horace. There is no boy to fetch faggots for the fire, or to take down the bottles 'pitched' in the Consulship of Manlius and then after dinner to send for either Phyllis or Chloe. There are no such amenities around here.

Part I

Early Days

It has been said that the pointing finger of Parnell is directed towards a public house and underneath is written that 'no man has a right to fix a boundary of the march of a nation'. I would prefer to think that finger is pointing towards the Rotunda where the nation continually marches on and where I was born on 18 January 1914. There is no plaque, but then plaques to the living are regarded as unlucky because, for one thing, they seem to carry with them the impediment of failing to get an overall majority.

I lived in Dublin, without any knowledge of it, where my father worked in the GPO or in Sherriff Street, for the first eighteen months of my life. Then my father and mother returned to their native Mayo where we settled on a small farm in the townland of Doolough, purchased from a local landlord called Carter, the same man who gave the land for the town of Belmullet, and where I was joined eventually by six siblings – two brothers and four sisters.

We were a very happy homestead and I was of an extremely enquiring nature from my earliest recall. I did not accept the popular myth that new babies were found under cabbage leaves or came in on the foam of the sea and accordingly carried out my own childish scientific examinations, both on the foam of the sea and under cabbage leaves. I found no child. The one remaining myth I had not explored was that it came in a doctor's bag.

One evening, I think I was aged about five, the Doctor arrived and left his bag in the hall while he went into the sitting room with my father to have their customary drink before he started attending to my mother, who was with child. Meanwhile I opened the bag and there was no baby there.

My childhood finished at that point because I was then able to combine this experience with my farmyard knowledge of animals to satisfy myself that birth was a natural process. Santa Claus vanished too. I had knowledge beyond my years. It was a knowledge though, that made me feel alone even if I secretly laughed at the expressed or implied innocence of my peers.

As a family we were never sure where we came from. Nor indeed did anybody try to find out. The only idea that I had from talking to my father was that we must have had cousins, pretty distant cousins, at Newcastle-Upon-Tyne. My father cycled from his home in Mayo in 1902 to Dublin, took the boat to Holyhead and cycled across England to Newcastle where he stayed with the family of William Lindsay for a fortnight or so. We never heard very much about that particular family from him, except for the fact that they were there.

Much later I discovered that a grandson of that particular William Lindsay, one Hugh Lindsay, became Bishop of Hexham and Newcastle from which office he has retired in the last year or so.

I have been in communication with him by reason of the fact that I knew a story about his Aunt Kathleen who was a singer of some sorts and certainly sang in the Opera House in Berlin. It was there she met a German doctor named Stoering, and ultimately married him. The story moves then to 1934 when I returned from University College Galway on holidays. My father was in a state of what might be described as 'heraldic emotion'. He had read a letter from the then Bishop of Killala, Dr James Naughton, who in turn, enclosed a letter he had received from Berlin from this Kathleen Lindsay-Stoering setting out certain names and places in Mayo related to her family. She wanted birth certificates, baptismal certificates, marriage certificates, in fact any kind of evidence that could be procured. It became quite clear then, not to me but to my father who was conversant with international affairs all his life, that Adolf Hitler was probably 'incinerator minded' in relation to Kathleen Lindsay-Stoering.

We searched all the local baptismal records and marriage records in various places and the only one of any consequence that we discovered was the baptismal record of Hugh Lindsay, in Westport Parish Church, 1824. We established that this Hugh Lindsay was the great grandfather of Bishop Hugh Lindsay and would have been the grandfather of Kathleen Lindsay-Stoering. Whatever papers we gathered together were sent back to the family in Newcastle, and they in turn got in touch with the relevant office in Edinburgh and, from the searches there, it emerged that a man called Hugh Lindsay who was the fifth son of the then Earl of Crawford and Balcarres, left Scotland sometime in the 1700s to find his fortune in Ireland. We could never ascertain what particular kind of business he pursued, but it is not beyond the bounds of possibility that his business was proselytising. Of that, of course, we are not sure.

From what we know, he went first to Kerry and later on moved up the coast to Louisburgh which is adjacent to Westport and would explain the baptism of Hugh Lindsay in Westport Parish, 1824. The fact that he was the fifth son of an Earl would not amount to very much. In a family like that, the first son would succeed to the title and the estates, the second son would go to the navy, the third son to the army and the fourth to the Church. There was nothing left for Hugh except Ireland. For whatever reason, he moved from the Westport area down through Ballycroy and finally settled on a very beautiful scenic hillside called Mount Jubilee, which is the village from which my father came before he settled in the townland of Doolough.

My mother's family name was Keegan. They came from some part of Co. Sligo, probably Easkey or Enniscrone. They were coastguards and lighthouse keepers and two of them settled down, one of them in the village of Duhoola which is in my home parish and the other in the village of Tahalanduff, near to the village of Geesala. Each ran small shops, groceries, household commodities and the like but I think both shops were run to earth by mismanagement and probably over-indulgence.

My mother had two other uncles, whose names I don't recall because I never saw them. They were both officers in the Merchant Navy and came home on holidays from time to time. One died in his chair after lunch, and the other died after tea in the evening, not of course on the same day. These two deaths played an important part in my life. At the age of twelve I was in secret communication with a British training ship situated at Conway in North Wales. I probably saw the advertisement for cadets in some paper or other and I was trying desperately to go to sea and get in at the right end without any advice whatsoever from anybody – not to mention seeking anybody's permission. The postal communication was intercepted and I was forbidden to have anything further to do with naval inclinations, because, as my mother said: 'Your two great uncles died suddenly at home'. I could never see the logic of this but in any event I may well have been saved from the perils of the sea by the example of two men who died at home in their comfortable chairs.

* * * *

We lived across a strand in the village of Geesala in the townland of Doolough. All our land had a coastline on an inlet of Blacksod Bay, ten miles south of Belmullet. The inlet was tidal and when the tide was out we generally ran across the strand for messages to the local shop in the village. In those days we could be sent up to twenty times a day, always barefoot. I didn't wear my first shoes – which I hated – until my confirmation.

I remember one day visiting, what were to me, very old people in a house in the village. Probably they were quite young – in their thirties, but then age is relative. On my journey I slipped while crossing a fence and fell onto a rusty piece of gate or plough, causing a very severe gash to my foot which resulted in heavy bleeding. The lady of the house came out, brought me into a cowhouse and applied fresh cow dung to the wound without washing it first. It was my first venture into antibiotics and years later when I asked her about it she explained that dung contained the equivalent of anti-tetanus because it was what was rejected as poison from the natural foods the animals ate.

I got into serious trouble when I arrived at home with a piece of woollen stocking tied around my foot, enclosing cow dung over the gash. However the efficacy of the treatment is proven by the fact that no scar ever formed.

It was from the same woman that I first heard the word 'soliloquise'. She said to me one day: 'A lot of people around here think I'm mad, because I do talk to myself, but I'm only soliloquising like Alexander Selkirk', I went home, where my mother was able to find in the dictionary the meaning of the word, but I had to wait until my father came home to find out who Alexander Selkirk was. He was able to recite the poem in its entirety:

I am monarch of all I survey
my right there is none to dispute
from the centre all round to the sea
I am lord of the fowl and the brute

Not very long after, I was about five at the time, there was a discussion at home as to the maiden name of the wife of the local landlord, Denis Bingham. I was hungry and getting somewhat impatient as the discussion continued and someone offered that she was formerly 'Miss Eager'. I interjected and said: 'Whatever her maiden name was, I'm very eager for my supper.' I think it was from that time that my father discovered I was interested in words and language, and he started to supply me with books which I believe he bought in secondhand bookshops in Ballina or from peddlers. Before I went away to secondary school I had read all of Macauley's essays, Charles Dickens, Kickham and several others. I can recall to this day, – without having read it since – what Macauley said in the course of his speech in the

House of Commons on the endowment of Maynooth: 'She (the Roman Catholic Church) may still exist in undiminished vigour when some traveller from New Zealand shall, in the midst of a vast solitude, take his stand on a broken arch of London Bridge to sketch the ruins of St Pauls.'

And so I became a reader.

Incidentally among my father's books I came across a hardback edition of *Lady Chatterley's Lover* (first published in 1928). I don't know where he got it. Many pages of it were covered in asterisks and I later realised that it was an expurgated edition, but I did have some prurient fun trying to supply letters for the asterisks. I haven't had as much fun with the crossword since.

* * * *

One evening I was sent across the strand on an unexplained message, to exchange a pound note for two ten shilling notes. I went to Geesala to Mrs Gaughan's shop, whose family are still there. I never heard her speak but she was always humming to herself. I asked her for my message and she handed me what I thought were two ten shilling notes. As I was returning home across the strand the tide began to come in and the early splash into the channel made me lose my grip on the notes and they fell into the water. However, I managed to recover them but I was afraid to go home as I felt I had committed some frightful wrong by allowing money to get wet. Later I was to discover that it was not such a great wrong to get money wet, it was a much greater wrong to get wet through the use of money! Having retrieved the money I endeavoured to dry it. I separated the notes and placed them on a stone wall and in doing so I found that there were **three**, not two ten shilling notes.

A great battle ensued by what was then believed to be, on the right and the left shoulder, the good angel and the bad angel. The battle was tense and long because, to a small boy, a ten shilling note was a fortune. But the good angel won and I returned to Mrs Gaughan and told her that she had given me three notes instead of two. She went on humming, took the three notes and gave me back two. She then uttered the only words I ever heard her say: 'Wait a minute'. She filled a big tea packet of bulls-eye sweets, a kindness she repeated every Friday evening on my way home from school.

* * * *

Only in later life is one privileged to observe in wonderment a mother's worth. I was so privileged being the eldest of seven surviving children.

On first observation it became clear that fathers of that era played no part whatever within the indoor domestic scene. And it must be remembered that I grew up during the period of the open fire, hand cleaning, hand washing, candles and oil lamps. Cooking for a family of nine on an open fire was no mean feat.

Work outdoors was in the main pursued by the father and the older male children. In fine weather everyone, both male and female took part in the hay saving, of all farm work undoubtedly the most pleasant. Turf, the only heating substance then available in rural Ireland, was cut by hand and saved in the successive processes of spreading, footing and gathering. It was finally taken near the home and stacked, with the whole family lending a hand. When finished, the turf stack was an object of great pride. Barely a sod was lost no matter how rainy the winter.

The same precision of workmanship applied to ricks of hay, to the stacking of oats and to the planting of root crops. A ridge or drill of potatoes presented even to the untrained eye, a work of art.

Such rural scenes have been preserved on the canvases of Charles Lamb and Paul Henry. It was an era when every rood of ground maintained its man. The milking of cows was hand done, mainly by women except when a particular cow proved to be contrary. The female of any species had a healthy respect for the male in those days! Curiously, the appreciation of the male in giving a hand – however insignificant it might have been, like the lifting of a heavy pot from the fire – commanded great respect from the women. It was a simpler time. Whether better is another question.

Children realised how important they were in the scheme of things when they were asked to place potato seeds or cabbage plants in the adult-prepared land. Being allowed to drive cattle from the sheds to the pasture was a position of some status, but for a child, it was not until one was asked to run a message to the shops or the post-office in the village that one really became an integral part of the household team.

We remained a team until we left home, married and started families of our own. The importance of this was demonstrated by the fact that even when we were grown-up most of our holidays and indeed many weekends, were spent at home. Home never ceases to be home. We in turn brought up our children to savour the delights of rural life.

* * * *

In a funny way, I regard the lack of recall of one's first year or two of life as something of a blessing. As I have mentioned, I was born in Dublin where my father and mother then lived after, I suspect, an elopement. There could have been no other reason for the mutual dislike, or worse, that manifestly existed between my maternal grandfather and my father. Years later, long after my grandfather had gone to his reward, when I included his name in those given to my son my father referred to his grandson as 'the child'.

My first memories recall all the features of rural bliss. The sun did not rise or set over chimney tops; we had the mountains and the sea. Snow in my childhood was an infrequent event; so was heavy frost or an icy road. There were sand roads then and the freezing of sand is something of which I have no scientific knowledge or actual experience. The odd stone jutting out of the sandy surfaces caused many a toe bruise to the unwary, barefooted child. That, and the occasional fall into a boghole, were the only hazards, and they were far from fatal.

The seasons differ in town and country but for sheer enjoyment the country wins, particularly for children. Spring could be harsh since it came after the joys of Christmas and school holidays. That, however, was only the beginning of spring. The days were becoming longer albeit imperceptibly, as the old Irish saying has it 'like the skip of a cock on a dunghill'. In my home district the growth to be seen was largely confined to heather and the grass reclaimed from rebellious land, mainly cut-away bog, the work of countless generations of earnest bread winners whose assiduity was never interrupted by conferences or seminars where economists now drone on about the theory of productivity and the necessary prelude to prosperity. And when the wild flowers or the young lambs frolicked their first steps, the people acknowledged nature's wonder by exclaiming: 'May we be alive this time next year.'

Summer heralded sunshine and further growth. The turf saving began with suitable intervals for each process, the cutting, the spreading, the footing and the gathering. Nowadays they begin to mow hay earlier. In my childhood it was believed that it should not be mown until 15 August. Whether properly or mistakenly, the view held was that the return would be best at that time. The great game was tumbling in the hay.

Autumn, immortalised by John Keats, was for me exactly what Keats described in his famous *Ode*. When I first read that exquisite poem not long after childhood had passed, I remembered the things applicable only to the wild western coast of Ireland. Curiously, I always remember autumn as a time of heavy rains, lightning and thunder storms. The tides appeared to be higher and at their lowest, the varying hues of seaweed – brown yellow and black – formed a great canvass underneath the blue skies and scudding clouds.

From my home I could see what seemed to me a vast mountain. It was Mount Jubilee Hill. As a child I climbed to its summit. That was an Everestian triumph.

On the side nearest my home was a foxes den into which we crawled. This I did several times, and found no fox. What if there had been one? No one thought of that because in the words of an old and dear neighbour, 'youth is brave'.

On another side of this hill was a monument, a relic of some ancient religious worship. Around it was a tiny graveyard where unbaptised children were interred. My still-born baby sister lies there. Here, on the feast of the Assumption local people made a miniature pilgrimage and the silence would be broken by the reciting of prayers. A few years ago a very beautiful church was constructed there. I was pleased to be at its opening with my old friends and neighbours.

The village of Mount Jubilee holds a special meaning for me. Here my father's family settled after their Scot's forbears wandered from Scotland via Kerry and finally settled in Mayo.

* * * *

At the age of four and a half I went to school. The school was in the village of Geesala, on the other shore of Blacksod Bay from where we lived at Doolough. So when I went to school I was a stranger. None of the other children knew me.

I shall never forget my first day at school. My father took me. On route he was kind and encouraging, stressing what a great time was in store for me. I listened, but was not impressed. At the entrance I refused to go any further and, bawling loudly, had to be carried inside. The principal teacher, a man I later recognised as somewhat aloof, was anxious to pacify me; he gave me a blue slate and a pencil of the same but softer material. These did not placate me. Now my misery was complete because my father had disappeared. The teacher then resorted to the successful ruse of placing me beside his niece, a blue-eyed beauty of three and a half. She smiled and that made me feel better. With the sleeve of my gansey I wiped the tears away and school thereafter was a different and infinitely more acceptable place.

Almost immediately we were transferred to the assistant teacher, who dealt with infants and one or two higher classes. Her name was Sarah Conway, later she became Sarah Gunning. We grew to be friends and continued as such until her death at a ripe old age.

In these times it is difficult to believe that, by the time I was six and a half, I partook of three sacraments on three consecutive days. Having made my First Confession on a Friday in June 1920, I received my First Holy Communion the next day; on the Sunday the Bishop made me a strong and perfect Christian. At least he thought he did. For myself I must confess that this tridiuum of spiritual *avoir-du-pois* weighed lightly indeed on my shoulders.

What was really exciting was the new suit, first necktie and boots that were, according to the economics of the era, too big for me; they were meant to last longer than three days and no doubt eventually be passed on to a younger brother. They did in fact last a long time because going barefoot was one of my joys, even in winter. Those were the days before tarmacadam and loose stones cut and damaged our toes.

Another event took place that Sunday. A picnic had been arranged in the front garden of the local Jubilee nurse's cottage by the parents and teachers. I don't recall any clerical presence. They were all in fact lunching with the Bishop while we sat on the grass, drinking lemonade and eating large semi-sweetened biscuits supplied by

Jacobs. Apart from the enjoyment the only residue were damp trousered backsides and snail tracks. The scene thus presented looked as if noses had been wiped on our little trousers and on the dresses of the little girls.

As a youngster, on my way home from school I took a keen interest in stealing carrots out of the fields. We had carrots at home but they never tasted as well as the carrots in other people's fields. They were especially nice when they were washed in sea water; that gave them a lovely tang. I used to watch the men working in the fields in the days before machinery. The only machinery I saw in my childhood was a spraying machine and I remember cycling five miles to see it, the men walking up and down spraying blue-coloured liquid on potato stalks. I was full of wonder at the courage of these men who tackled up to two acres with a spade in the damp cold October weather. At this time two spades were in use; one was a two-rivet spade and the other was a three-rivet spade. The rivets were driven into the spade handle and it took a real man to use the three-rivet spade; lesser mortals used the two-rivet. They would start to dig and break up the soil, moving along without markers yet managing to work in very straight lines. They wore belted coats and hats or caps. The work was slow, not causing warmth or a rush of blood and they would rest every 10 or 15 yards.

I often wondered what they were thinking about as they leaned on their spades and stared out to sea. Sometimes they might turn and look at a heron, or a crane, or a seagull. These men often told me that when the seagulls came inland it was a sign of bad weather.

This part of Mayo suffered the curse of emigration because the holdings were uneconomic. It was something that would play a part in my political life at a later stage in relation to unemployment assistance for small holders, the bringing into existence of which I approved but the implementation of which I did not approve, but more on that later. The saddest thing of my childhood was to watch families or parts of families going away to Scotland for the potato picking or harvesting.

Some of my class-mates had to leave before they finished school, and were it not for my mother and father and the sacrifices they were prepared to make, I would have had to leave too. I read the novels of Patrick MacGill in later years and they echoed my own thoughts and feelings on emigration.

* * * *

Geesala was a small and simple village, no different from any other village of its size. There were no semi-detached houses that stood in their own grounds. There were a few shops, the priest's house, the teacher's house, the post-office and three pubs.

I will always remember the first motor-car which came to the village. It had been bought by a new curate from Belmullet, Fr David Donoghue, who wouldn't, ordinarily have been able to own a motor-car except that he came from a wealthy family. He took the precaution of sending a young man, Michael Barrett, who had just finished school to Josie Burke's garage in Castlebar for three months, to learn all about the workings of the engine. I remember the night he came back well. There was a great gathering to see the car. He also had little presents for the rest of us, wonderful things, magic things that could lift pins and nails. They were magnets, which I had never seen before. You could take pins out of woman's hair at Mass. They eventually led to mischief and trouble.

At the crossroads in Geesala was a very distinctive but not much frequented pub. It was owned by John McGeehin, who came to our part of the country as the principal of Geesala National School. Before that he had been principal teacher of a school in Donegal, I think Annagry. However, for some reason which we never discovered he had been sacked from that position.

After his dismissal he spent a number of years in Recess working at the old railway station on the Galway-Clifden line. He never spoke about his time there.

John McGeehin became the principal of Geesala National School because there was no communication between the parish priest of wherever he came from in Donegal and our parish priest. He didn't survive very long as a teacher in Geesala – he was sacked for assaulting his predecessor, a man called Cauldwell, who was the great grandfather of Sean Gunning who later built the 'Ostan Synge' in Geesala – the bar of which I had the great honour of officially opening in 1986.

McGeehin later owned the post-office and lost it. He then acquired the public house at the crossroads, which to my great dismay is now called the 'High Chaparral'.

McGeehin then built a dance hall. It was fully equipped with a bar and had an unusual feature which I'm sure no other dance hall had: a show window in which were displayed ladies' evening dresses, men's dinner jackets and shoes for both sexes which could be hired at a very modest rate. I don't think he did a great business from that window, because everybody knew where a particular suit or dress had come from.

But McGeehin had tremendous dances there. People travelled from all over the country and, if the dance was on a Friday night, you might well see some of the dancers departing on the following Monday.

McGeehin always made a speech at every dance and started proceedings by dancing with his current barmaid who, according to local gossip, was rather more intimate than a barmaid. The last one, I recall, became a parish priest's housekeeper in the Midlands.

John McGeehin was really a showman before his time – a sort of P.T. Barnum, a great advertiser. The posters he had for the dances were something else. He used to invite people to his 'banqueting hall' – this wasn't any old dance hall – 'where you could mingle in the terpsichorean art with people from as far away as the Royal College of Surgeons in the East, to University College Galway in the West, from Donegal in the North, to Limerick in the South'.

Now the East was represented by a medical student from the parish attending the Royal College of Surgeons in Dublin; I was the sole representative of UCG; the Donegal representatives were McGeehin's nephews and nieces; and the Limerick people were acquaintances of one of the barmaids.

At one stage he started a corn-grinding mill and a co-operative, but the people did not support him because they felt he was making too much money out of it. The Irish are sometimes called 'a nation of begrudgers', I don't think the accusation is too far off the mark. We are ready and willing to help a neighbour up to his own shoulder height but as soon as he shows signs of going any higher he is promptly stopped.

Johnny McGeehin never allowed a dance to finish without making a speech. He was a very fine public speaker and had been a member of Mayo County Council for a number of years. In spite of being highly unpopular he was very respected by reason of his ability and it was this which got him elected. The speeches he made at country dances always caught my fancy and many a time I quoted him afterwards. Johnny used to thank everybody for coming even people who were not there. 'I must make special mention of the ladies,' he would say, 'their beauty and their dresses. The ladies, I think to myself, are like the stars. The stars are the poetry of heaven. The ladies, are the poetry of earth.' No one knew it better than Johnny did.

As soon as McGeehin became involved in the dance hall he became a target for the clergy who regarded dancing and drinking as an occasion of sin and waged a non-stop war against him and his hall. Peculiarly enough, years later McGeehin sold the property to the clergy and it became a parish hall.

I was very friendly with McGeehin, although he and my father hated one another. It was, I think, because he had blocked my father in a monitorship for teaching that my father never forgave him. They used to engage in correspondence through the local paper, berating each other, much to the enjoyment of all the neighbours. It helped to sell the *Western People* in the area.

I recall the St Stephen's night I went around to the dance hall, which was now being run by the clergy. I was home from UCG for the Christmas holidays. I had saved the seven shillings and sixpence for the dance by getting a lift from Ballina and travelling on the back of a lorry to Geesala.

But before parting with my money I decided to take a look inside the hall. The men were all on one side, the girls on the other – total segregation. Sitting under the band which had come from Belmullet, were the parish priest and the curate, and at the door was a sergeant and one of the guards. I decided it was not the kind of scene in which I should invest any money, and that dividends would not be forthcoming either through dancing, or anything that might subsequently occur. So I wandered up to McGeehin's pub. His latest barmaid was there and I ordered myself a pint. Then there came a shout from the kitchen:

'Who's there?'

'Pat Lindsay,' the barmaid replied.

'Which of them – the young Pat or the old Pat?'

'Young Pat'.

'Tell *him* to come up.' The him was accentuated.

So I carried my pint up to the kitchen; sitting in front of a roaring fire was John McGeehin with his one eye. He had lost an eye in a shoot-out during the Civil War. I think it was the only Civil War shot fired in my part of the country. The lost eye made him somewhat forbidding, but he was in other respects, a good looking man.

'Tis a wonder you're not at the dance?'

'Where's the dance, Mr McGeehin?'

'Is there not a dance in the hall?'

'No, I looked in. It is neither a dance nor a wake. It is that awful moment before death when everyone is on tip-toe.'

With that he shouted to the barmaid below: 'Bring up another pint and bring me a bottle of Redbreast.'

He was delighted with my news that the priests weren't doing well in the hall. Later I graduated from the pint to the Redbreast. I had a wonderful night and still had my seven and sixpence, less of course the price of the first pint – ten old pence.

We discussed a lot of matters that night, including the whole question of Masses for the dead. I was conscious that John had something on his mind and he eventually put the vital question: 'Would you be able to tell me, from your learning of apologetics and other subjects, of what greater value would £500 for Masses at an honourarium of £1 per Mass be over, one Mass at a greater honourarium?'

At the back of my mind I knew that somewhere there was a will, and that the priest had probably got back the price of the dance hall in the Mass offerings to be claimed from John, after his death.

My reply, which might not have been too sound theologically, was good enough for my purpose in relation to the bottle of Redbreast. I told McGeehin that if Christ on Calvary had saved the souls of the whole world and the Mass being the reincarnation of Calvary, then I couldn't see why one Mass couldn't save a soul.

Once again McGeehin raised his voice in the direction of the bar: 'Miss, bring me my writing-box.' A box was produced and out of it he took a will and there, sure enough, was the stipulation for £500 for Masses at an honorarium of £1 per Mass.

We chatted a little longer about this particular subject. The outcome was the addition of a codicil to the will – cancelling the £500 and leaving £25 for a Requiem Mass and £25 for the Month's Mind Mass. The only mistake we made was that there were no others present. The barmaid and I witnessed the codicil.

As a result, when the will was ultimately produced the priests knew that I was the instigator of the change and the author of the codicil. But I had saved John McGeehin £450 which his nephews and nieces ultimately got.

He donated a plot of ground as a graveyard and when he died in the mid 1940s he was buried in the most prominent part of that graveyard. To this day nobody has put a tombstone on his grave. He lies in an unmarked grave.

* * * *

As a youngster I had a tendency to follow a coffin at a funeral without knowing where it was going. During the wake which was an integral part of life in those days, I was invariably asked to say the Rosary at a certain time during the night. There was a bonus for that – you were brought to a room and given whisky or poteen. The ordinary mourners at the wake had to do with very flat stout. I think I lost the job because I did not have a Rosary beads and used to use the railings on the back of a kitchen chair to count the decades. There were a few occasions when a decade might be twelve, or other occasions when there might be only eight Hail Marys. Gradually my services were no longer sought.

* * * *

Life in our village was simple. We visited houses and had card playing sessions. I was often an interested spectator watching ten men playing 'twenty five' – five sets of partners. Often a rumpus would start after a round because some fellow's partner had not played the deuce of diamonds or the five of spades. This card playing was taken very seriously. People had reputations as good card players and it was something not to be treated lightly.

Another form of entertainment was the school dance. Why it was called the school dance I am not sure, because it didn't take place in a school but in different houses and would run for about ten nights. The cost of the dance was about a shilling and you got tea and currant cake. You danced and you did the best you could to 'get off' with one or other of the girls there.

I remember once going with a great friend of mine, John Clapham from Achill, to the Protestant social in Dugort run by the local sub post-mistress. It was frequented by as many Catholics as Protestants. Dugort was a great little Protestant colony – colonised by a Rev. Mr Nangle in the mid-nineteenth century. They had their own hospital, their own printing press, and their own newspaper *The Achill Herald*, some copies of which still exist.

Off to the social we went. We picked out two lovely sisters whom we knew were just home from England. We danced with them for the night and eventually put to them the vital question: 'Could we see you home?' They agreed. We went along the strand towards the village of Dooniver, but were too bashful to tell them that we were hoping for a little canoodling.

However our hopes rose when a shower of rain suddenly started and this gave us the excuse to shelter at each end of a turf stack. John and I both suffered the same fate – we were put on our backs after the first false move. The sisters twisted our arms, kneed us and threw us on the deck.

We only discovered afterwards that our lights of love were two sisters on holidays from Holloway jail where they were wardens, well skilled in all the arts of karate.

John's mother asked the neighbours afterwards: 'Have you heard the delightful story about how the girls from Dooniver dealt with Lindsay and our John?'

* * * *

I've mentioned already the lady who used soliloquise and who introduced me to Alexander Selkirk. She was the wife of Michael Heneghan who, in later years when I was a student, I used to shave every Friday. It was the time of the open or 'cut-throat' razor, when few older men shaved more than once or twice a week. It was quite common among older men that they did not shave themselves, they would either go to a barber or, more rarely, have a neighbour do the job, as in my case.

For this I received 20 cigarettes – one tenth of his pension. On a few occasions I was shameless enough to waylay him on his way back from the post-office for a pint as well. This of course was when I was a student at UCG. Such were the manoeuvres which students had to undertake in order to survive and enjoy themselves.

One day, as I was shaving Michael he asked me if I read a lot. I told him: 'Yes, I have read a lot, I'm reading a lot and I hope to continue to read a lot all of my life.'

'Well' he asked me, 'in all the reading did you hear of anybody coming back from what they call the Great Beyond?'

'No Michael, I didn't.'

'Lindsay' he said, 'I'm going to tell you something now. If you live as long as I am, or older, and you stay on reading you will never read of anybody coming back from the Great Beyond and I will tell you why – there is no Great Beyond.'

I thought this was rather strange in view of his age (he was almost 80 then) and death couldn't have been that many years away. So I began to study him. He used to attend 11 o'clock Mass every Sunday and would stand under the gallery. He would not make a sign of the cross, genuflect, or beat his breast. He would take no part in the proceedings, except to watch his neighbours with a degree of contempt as they came down from the communion rails. I could feel in my bones that he was picking out the hypocrites.

I took the opportunity once of asking him about his stance at last Mass. He answered: 'They're all hypocrites, except Maire hAnroi.'

I started to take notice of her after that and there was no doubt about it. She wore her shawl back on her greying hair and her unwrinkled brow was an absolute plateau of piety.

She was a great friend of mine and she came into my life again in an extraordinary way. In my part of the country at that time we were living in what might be described as primitive conditions. We had sandy roads, no tarmacadam. The sandy roads often became flooded and had little rivulets from the rain. But the most important rivulet I can recall was caused by the use of gable-ends as urinals when drinking was heavy. Drinking as a rule wasn't that heavy in my village even though there were three pubs there when I was growing up. Only the people who had some kind of income took a drink and it was taken moderately, usually on Friday evenings.

Traditionally in the month of May, gaffers descended from Scotland, gathering squads for potato picking. They drank from morning till night. They didn't have to go around recruiting very much as the people were so anxious to get into the squads, in order to get money together for Christmas that they sought these gaffers out.

While they were drinking in one particular pub they visited the gable quite frequently, sometimes singly and other times en masse. So on this particular day the gable was over used and this caused a rivulet across the sandy road. I was coming down the street, aged nine or ten at the time, and Maire was coming in the opposite direction. As she crossed the rivulet she lifted her long skirt and said: 'Pat, nuair a bhíonn an tól istigh bíonn níos mó ná an ciall amuigh.'

I carried on, quite amused with this remark and when I thought of it later it occurred to me that here was a perfect example of the only woman singled out for piety by Michael Heneghan. To the pure all things are pure.

* * * *

I remember about 1928. It was Easter. There was a mission taking place in the home church in Kiltane conducted by Jesuits. One, a rather senior man called Fr Mackey came out on to the altar. I remember vividly that he intoned himself in the typical Jesuit intimation of the Sign of the Cross, and then, with outstretched hand, he looked at the congregation and said: 'Along the valley of Cedron, down the slopes of Olivet there echoed the voice of Lucifer saying: "*Non serviam, Non serviam!*"'

I had just happened to have finished the third conjugation in Latin and I knew that *non serviam* meant 'I will not serve' and with the possible exception of the curate, I was the only one in the whole church who understood its meaning. It has often occurred to me since that that particular reference had a special meaning to me over the years as I now recognise Lucifer, and this is not a compliment to Lucifer, as the first subversive.

I remember on another occasion, a mission in the same church and my father asking a much older man what he thought of the sermon. The old man replied: 'Tis long and many a day since I first read that sermon in Fr Tom Burke's book.' They were talking about the famous preacher. One got away with very little in the West of Ireland in those days.

* * * *

There were wonderful characters around in my young days, philosophers, talkers and people who were great at making up yarns. I recall one evening being sent to the village to bring my father home. That meant separating Dr Callaghan and himself. I noticed that, as usual, neither was listening to the other (something my friends say about me from time to time). Yarn was following yarn and, while one was telling one anecdote, the other was thinking up another to follow. They were very good, clean and almost innocent yarns, and in all of them, there was an element of truth, so it was extremely hard not to believe them.

This particular evening my father was telling a story which Dr Callaghan swallowed holus polus. He told the doctor that one evening he was down at the end of his holding of land; there was a rock which the sea covered at full tide, but sometimes a little bit of it jutted up above the water. My father noticed that a rat was attacking a barnacle but he couldn't shift it. As the tide came in, the rat reversed up the part that was sticking out of the water. Meanwhile as the barnacle became covered by the incoming tide, and with the rat out of the way, it loosened its grip on the rock. The rat waited until the tide had gone out again, moved down near the barnacle and piddled on it. The barnacle thought that the tide was in again, relaxed its grip on the rock, and was devoured by the rat.

* * * *

There was extraordinary rivalry among the doctors at that time. Our two local doctors, Dr Conway in Belmullet and Dr Callaghan in Bangor Erris both came from within a few doors of each other in George's Street in Newport Co. Mayo. They did not speak to one another.

And then a marvellous man came along and set up practice in Belmullet. Dr Thomas Kelly really wiped out the practices of the other two and they finished up as glorified midwives. Anyway, they rarely read their medicine.

On one occasion Dr Kelly sent my mother in to the Richmond Hospital to Dr Adam McConnell, one of the great brain surgeons of Europe in those years. My mother had suffered a partial stroke. I was in Belmullet and hadn't yet finished at the Bar, so Dr Kelly told me that when I got back to Dublin I was to go and see McConnell and tell him certain things about my mother, especially concerning her speech and limb movements.

Dr McConnell received me in his rooms in Fitzwilliam Square and I did my best to carry out Dr Kelly's instructions. In the course of our conversation he remarked: 'Do the people of your area realise the great blessing they have in having a man like Dr Kelly, who is the best diagnostician I have ever come across?' I never told Dr Kelly that but I did tell his widow.

Mrs Kelly taught at national school for many years and is the mother of some very distinguished medical men, Vivian in Jervis Street, Joe in the Orthopaedic section at Merlin Park and another son Desmond in general practice in Westport.

The loyalty to doctors in those days in rural Ireland was incredible. People would not change doctors even for the benefit of the patient. I remember once my father hiding when my mother summoned Dr Kelly because he did not want to appear to be a party to any disloyalty to his drinking friend Dr Callaghan. Yet but for Dr Kelly my sister would have died of fever.

The same level of loyalty existed between neighbours and towards tradesmen. My mother once asked a fellow to put a chimney stack on our house. He got his moulds, took the timber off, and then brought her outside to show it to her. She said 'That is upside down.' His reply disarmed her: 'Every fault,' he said, 'is a fashion, ma'am.'

There was one great tradesman in our area, a man by the name of Ned Doocey. His children went to school with me. Ned was partial to a 'little drop'. My father visited him once when he was sick and Ned asked what he thought would be good for him. My father replied, 'Plenty of buttermilk'.

When my father had left Ned said to his wife: 'Mary dear, if Patrick was suffering as I am suffering, it's not buttermilk he'd drink. Would you ever go down to the village and fetch me a noggin?'

Ned Doocey was a lovable and an inoffensive man. He sang one song, 'Down in Kilkenny where the marble stones are as black as ink'. My father who was a good violinist also had one song, ' Two little girls in blue' and was in good demand to sing it.

Anytime my father would return from the pub a bit merry he had another ditty. In later years I thought it was like 'Abbeyfeale Abbeyfeale' because it was so repetitive. It was a form of appeasement of my mother whose face would be unsmiling on these occasions and it was 'Don't be angry, I was only teasing you'.

The song would be repeated because my father hoped to get a smile but he never succeeded.

* * * *

I have always hated violence, in part because of a sad event in my own childhood.

On 15 November 1924, a neighbour passing on his way to the fair in Belmullet came in to our house and put a revolver, and some bullets in a matchbox on the over mantel in the sitting-room. He was obviously afraid to carry them. This may have been because of his fear of being arrested or some other reason I didn't understand at the time. Guns were fairly plentiful in those days, in the immediate aftermath of the War of Independence and the Civil War. In any event, he warned me not to touch them.

The over mantel was high but not too high for me and he hadn't gone a 100 yards before I was up on a chair. I was loading and reloading the gun and eventually I didn't know whether it was loaded or not. My little brother John, then aged about four and a half, got up on a baby chair outside the window and looked in to see what I was doing in a locked room.

I pulled back the curtain, pointed the revolver at him, hoping to frighten him with a 'click'. The gun was loaded. The bullet went in over his eye and lodged in his head quite close to his brain. He was rushed to the Richmond Hospital in Dublin under the care of the late Sir Thomas Myles who advised against extraction. He urged care and especially the avoidance of falls. But that is precisely what happened.

In 1936 when he was seventeen he fell off a bicycle and the bullet moved, causing what was immediate epilepsy and death within a few days.

Now, like every young person, one gets over grief very fast. So when I went to university I joined the Officers Training Corps. It was the fashion at the time. We got lovely uniforms, Sam Brown belts and maroon and white epaulettes, the colour of UCG. We got in addition £8 a year and spent a fortnight in Finner Camp. The first two thirds was paid the Monday after arrival and the remainder was paid when we left.

I remember at Finner being brought to the rifle range and I fired one shot. Immediately the smell of the cordite brought the whole tragic event back to me. I didn't, and I couldn't fire any more.

I hate guns and violence and I am appalled at grown-up mature people behaving in a sub-human fashion. And I am appalled too at the sadness of it all, at the fact that an awful lot of these people who engage in murder are, in other respects, very able and intelligent. But they have allowed the sub-human to conquer their intelligence and thus deprive their families and their communities of their presence and their talents.

In later years I prosecuted in the Special Criminal Court and while I did my job firmly but fairly I was always sad to see talented young men and women going off to serve, in most instances, very long sentences. What a waste!

* * * *

Saint Muredach's

My father knew that ten scholarships for Mayo County Council were awarded to people to attend secondary school and that they were eagerly sought and much coveted. I well remember changing from Geesala National School to Doolough because my father felt there was a better teacher there. She wasn't a better teacher but she had more enthusiasm and she came to our home in the evenings to prepare me for the scholarship examination. Mrs Sheridan is a woman to whom I shall always be grateful – she has long since gone to her reward. Before her marriage she was Miss Corkery from Sliabh Glas which is just outside Castlegregory in Co. Kerry. She was absolutely wonderful and wore herself out for her pupils. She married a very decent man, Hugh Sheridan a first cousin of John D. Sheridan, whose humourous articles in the *Irish Independent* gave me pleasure for many years.

Early in 1927 my father built me a bicycle. I only realise now what a remarkable man he was. He would buy spokes and rims and build bicycle wheels. He could sole and heel shoes and give haircuts. He could cure milk-fever in cows and was sent for, like a doctor or a priest, in the middle of the night. He always went. He wrote letters for people, and yet for all the letters he wrote and read for others he never betrayed a confidence, not even to my mother.

At any event, in Easter 1927 my father and I set off and cycled for 45 miles to Castlebar for my scholarship examination. We had a meal in Mulranny of bread, butter and jam and lots of strong tea. In Castlebar we stayed in lodgings on Main Street and my father passed the time there while I sat the examination.

The only person I recall taking part in the exam with me, and indeed he got first place, was the former Archbishop of Tuam, Dr Joseph Cunnane.

The exam over, we cycled home and eventually I heard that I had been successful and had won a scholarship. This, in turn, led me on 4 September 1927 to Ballina where I had never been before. On that date I started my secondary schooling at St Muredach's College. My father and mother came with me. It was a big event in their lives. It was a very big event in my life also, but it did not register as such, because I well recall sitting on my bed that night and beginning to count ... September, October, November, December. Would I ever see home again?

Well, I did go home again that Christmas. But after my time in the college, which was the biggest building I had ever been in, everything seemed smaller. My brothers and sisters seemed smaller and so did my mother and father. Even our house was smaller. It was an extraordinary effect which has been experienced by almost everybody who goes away to boarding school.

On that first journey to Ballina while my mother went off shopping my father brought me to what turned out to be a public meeting. It was the final rally in Ballina prior to the September 1927 General Election and the principal speaker on the platform was W.T. Cosgrave. Somehow or other I felt, while listening to this frail little man with a quiff in his hair, speaking of affairs of the country which I, of course did not understand, that there was a sadness, a sad prophetic tone in his voice as to what might ultimately happen in this country.

That was my second political experience. My first was, I felt at the time, a rather tragic affair. My father was a strong supporter of the Irish Parliamentary Party and he had no time for Sinn Feiners which included, of course, Mr Cosgrave, whom he later accepted with all the customary zeal of the convert. One Sunday after Mass there were men parading at home. They were wearing green, white and gold sashes, and one of them, a friend of mine took me by the hand. That was in 1917, I was three years old and I marched up and down the village as a Sinn Feiner. I was hammered for it when I got home.

* * * *

When we first acquired a wireless it was for the sole use of my father. It came with earphones and used dry and wet batteries. My father got all the news but seldom shared it with anybody. My mother hated this performance because we all had to stay silent while he was listening to what the rest of us couldn't hear.

* * * *

I settled in quickly at St Muredach's, and before long I acquired somewhat of a reputation as an actor and impersonator. One of my favourite roles was taking-off the Bishop who was a frequent visitor to the college. I would frequently play the part of the Bishop calling the boys to come and collect their prizes on prize day. It was obviously a success as usually there was great clapping and cheering and encouragement to keep going. One particular day I was at this when I noticed that my audience's enthusiasm had waned considerably. I looked around and there was the Bishop, Dr Naughton, and the President listening attentively.

'Get up to my room' said the President, Monsignor O'Boyle. 'No' said Dr Naughton, 'let's sit here. I think the punishment that we will inflict is that we will get him to do it again.'

I did it again and neither of them held it against me.

Many years later, on the night when the past pupils of St Muredach's were presenting a portrait in oils to Dr O'Boyle on his elevation to the Bishopric of Killala I told that story to demonstrate what a gentleman he was.

* * * *

It was forbidden for us to go into Ballina without permission but I blithely ignored this rule and did so almost openly. I adopted the simple expedient of walking from the college into the town by the direct route – straight down the avenue and taking no covert action whatsoever. If I met a priest I simply explained that another priest had granted permission. I spoke this lie one day and was found out, so I was forbidden from going to Ballina for anything.

However, as luck would have it, the annual sports day was soon to take place and the bicycle race was the only sporting activity in which I had any interest. This was especially so since there was a £5 prize for the winner. My dilemma was that I had no bicycle and could not go into town to borrow one unless I had permission.

Undaunted, I climbed the stairs and knocked on the President's door. He opened it, in what I can only describe as a soutaned whirlwind and asked:'What do you want?'

'May I go to town to borrow a bicycle for the bicycle race, Sir?'

'You may *not* go to town now, or again, for that or any other purpose' and the door was banged in my face.

I had been grossly thwarted and was very annoyed. On my way back down the stairs I noticed, sticking out from under the stairs, the reflector light of a green Raleigh bicycle. I decided to 'borrow' it. I rode it in the bicycle race which I won easily, despite the fact that the machine had a heavy 3-speed gear. Afterwards Monsignor O'Boyle presented me with a brown envelope containing the £5. He did not advert to the fact that he had refused me permission to go to town; nor did he ask me where I got the bicycle – although he must have recognised it as his own.

Many years afterwards when I was a guest of the Monsignor's for dinner, after I had joined the Western Circuit as a barrister, he regaled me with all the stories which I thought he never knew of, during my time in St Muredach's.

* * * *

When I left Ballina with my Leaving Cert I also had with me a glowing reference to the Dean of Religion at UCG. The last sentence struck me as being very significant: 'He is always devoted to his religious duties.' I felt the proper interpretation of that was: 'Watch this fellow; he is likely to stray.'

As stray I did. On my arrival at UCG mindful of the compulsory nature of the religious enforcement in St Muredach's, I chose as my Dean of Residence the local Church of Ireland rector in Galway, knowing full well that he would not bother me. That worked for eight or nine months until it was discovered by Dean Hynes – about whom more later.

* * * *

The five years I spent in St Muredach's were happy though turbulent ones. The regime was strict. We rose at seven, washed, shaved and dressed. Some of us shaved at an earlier age than others. Fellows who were already shaving when they came to St Muredachs were not looked upon with favour by Dr O'Boyle. He regarded them (correctly) as prospective trouble makers. I remember one fellow coming in and he was not alone shaving but when he came to the college in the middle of Hilary term in 1932 he asked for, and got, a day off and set out on his bicycle. It was much later that we found out that he had gone home to his local polling booth in Co. Sligo to vote for Fianna Fáil. He eventually became a priest and is alive in some part of America. Obviously such a man was never meant for the Diocese of Killala.

* * * *

Some strange characters went through St Muredach's. One was before my time but he became a legend in the college. This was Dean Gilroy, now retired, from the parish of Belmullet. He should, if the Holy Ghost had been performing properly, have been the Bishop of Killala but other matters intervened. He was thought to be the brightest man who had gone to Maynooth from the Diocese of Killala.

* * * *

Some pupils were sent to St Muredach's largely to be smoothed out a bit, not necessarily to be educated. The then Bishop, Dr Naughton, used to refer to the people who came from my part of the country as 'the rough diamonds from Erris'. We were rough, but at least he called us 'diamonds'.

At prize-giving day before Christmas, Dr Naughton always began, by wishing us all a 'Happy Christmas' and concluded by wishing us a 'Holy and Happy vacation'. We certainly knew it would be happy, but we were very determined it would not be holy. Holiness at that stage was virtually compulsory, and the one great fault I found with religious observance at the college was this compulsory nature. One was expected to go to the communion rails every day of the week. If one didn't, the central intelligence agency, composed of two nuns kneeling on *prie'dius* behind us, noted the absentees and duly conveyed the information to the Dean of Studies. Those who did not receive communion were seen as potential trouble makers, not properly suited for the religious life.

There was a change of nun on one occasion. She was very small in stature and was responsible for cleaning the oratory, arranging the flowers and dusting the statues. Having no step ladder, she was unable to reach the tops of the statues, so I was commissioned as her assistant to dust them down. I have to say that I did not do it as a measure of any kind of adoration; I did it because I knew it would be followed by tea and excellent buns. That kind of material objective governed my school life, even my approach to the learning of religious knowledge. In fact I got first prize every year for religious knowledge. It took the form of a £5 note, a considerable sum of money in those days. I won it not because of any strong religious ardour; it was due entirely to a good memory and a shortage of money!

* * * *

The best characters of all arrived mid-term (usually because they had been expelled from another school).

I remember in particular on one cold February day, a new boy coming in wearing grey flannel trousers, a blazer and open neck shirt. This type of attire was frowned upon by the authorities. Once, when I tried to lengthen my time in bed one morning by wearing, instead of a pyjama top, a black polo-neck shirt which would save me time in dressing after I got up, I was approached by the President who asked: 'When is she going out?'

'I don't understand you Father'.

'I mean the bloody ship you're on! Get that gansey off and get into your collar and tie.'

This new boy arrived dressed as I have described, but next morning he too was wearing a collar and tie. We gathered round him. His name was Edward MacAndrew from Ballycroy. He was a bit of a curiosity because of his dress and the time of his arrival. In the course of questioning, he cast a rather meaningful look at me and asked: 'Would you be Lindsay?'

'I am.'

'I had two pints with your father in Mulranny last Friday' he said. Immediately I decided that he was a person to be cultivated and looked after; anybody who could afford two pints must be in possession of some amount of money.

Later that same day he enquired of me: 'Would it be possible to get a drink or two any evening here?'

'It's possible' I replied, 'but highly dangerous'.

I explained that after tea we would have about half an hour for such a purpose before the next study began at 8 o'clock, but that it was fraught with danger because we would be sitting in study with the Dean walking around, and the Dean could hardly fail to smell drink unless he had taken something himself. 'Ah,' he said, 'what the hell about it.' 'Where'll we go?' I replied. So we crept down by the trees on the left of the college as it faced the river Moy, and went into Ryder's pub.

The owner of the pub was George Ryder, a particular friend of my father. He, in fact was the father of Eva Philbin, who later became Professor of Chemistry at UCD. From the first time I met her, in a blue gym tunic when she was attending the Convent of Mercy in Ballina, until the day she retired, and indeed since then, she never changed one iota. She deserved success because it never went to her head.

Well, there we were in Ryders, in the bar which was behind a velvet curtain. We ordered, or at least my friend ordered, two pints. He took out an oval mustard tin box, a Colmans box I think. He inserted a finger and wound out a £5 note. It was the fashion at the time to keep money in one of these mustard tin boxes and my new friend's box was clearly well filled. I was right to believe that this was a person to be cultivated, because that mustard box must have contained at least £100. He must have 'borrowed' it from his father's till at home.

This particular fellow had never gone to a national school. He always set out for school in the morning but instead of arriving went to various houses where he played cards all day. When he was asked by Fr Harte, who was inflicted upon us as Dean of Studies after Fr Forde had left, to say the 'Our Father' in Irish, he could not. Possessed of some kind of intuition Fr Harte, who came from the Galway diocese, then asked: 'Do you know it in English?'

He did not. He knew nothing.

Another chap came from Newport, Co. Mayo. Despite the fact that he lived in the Tuam diocese he came to St Muredach's because his brother was a dispensary doctor in the Killala diocese. The following November he and my philantropic friend and myself were expelled. Strictly speaking we weren't so much expelled as that we decided to leave the college before we were expelled.

The circumstances surrounding our trouble were somewhat bizarre. The Newport chap had a habit of keeping a diary in which he inserted so many lies that one could not regard him as anything but a pathological liar. Maybe, putting it more kindly, he was a 'Walter Mitty' type but whatever he was, when the diary fell into the hands of the authorities all three of us found ourselves heavily incriminated. The activities ranged from drink, to women and any of the other forbidden fruits of the day or the night. When we were confronted with this we left – I can't remember why. But we came back the following afternoon.

The doctor's brother, the diarist, was expelled that evening and my friend of the oval piggy-bank and I slept in a room that was kept for those with illnesses. We were brought two wonderful meals by the nun whom I used to help clean the statues. My friend being of a suspicious cast of mind, refused to eat his meal because he insisted that it had been poisoned, so I ate the two dinners. The following afternoon he was taken away by his parents, never to return.

Later that same day my parents called. After some time I was summoned to the visitor's parlour. Dr O'Boyle addressed me: 'Your father and mother and I have decided that this is no place for you. Your proper place is in Canada or Africa... someplace where you can be dealing with wild animals and wild people. Goodbye, boy! I wish you luck in the world.'

'I am totally innocent of the charges against me,' I replied, 'but I want to thank you for your kindness to me during my stay here.' Politeness probably paid off in the end.

We left on a Thursday afternoon and that night I suffered agonies at home, not only from the tirades of my father and mother, but also from the jibing of my younger brothers and sisters. Friday came, and I spent a lonely day at home. On Saturday the local curate called to see my father and the two of them went off to Ballina. I heard later that Fr Finnerty, my Latin teacher, had written to the curate who came from the same part of the county, Moygowna, north of Crossmolina, asking the two of them to come to Ballina to see the President. When my father returned that night he knew – or felt he knew – far more about my misdemeanours than he had two days before. He accused me of the most serious of offences, throughout all of which I maintained a stony silence. Eventually my mother realised that there was nothing more my father had to say to me and she said: 'Go to bed and be up in time for Mass in the morning.'

'I have been wronged.'

'Just what are you going to do?' she asked.

'I am going into Belmullet to see the local rector and I will be in a good school within a week and I will be in Trinity next October.'

I went to bed and I did not go to Mass the following morning. The curate arrived again to see my father and the two of them went back to Ballina.

The following Tuesday I received a letter from the college President: 'Dear Pat, you are welcome to come back. I hope you will continue to be sober and industrious. Yours sincerely, P. O'Boyle.'

Naturally I went back to the school and to his great credit the President never referred to the matter again, but I am convinced to this day that my threat to 'take the soup' had an immediate effect on the powers-that-be in Ballina.

So I continued my studies because it was important to do a good Leaving Cert so that I could qualify for further County Council Scholarships. This I managed to do and I also managed to win a University Scholarship on the basis of my Leaving Cert.

* * * *

The quality of teaching in St Muredach's was uneven. Our English teacher, Fr John Murphy, a native of Ardnaree was, like the President, a brilliant linguist. His insistence on good grammar and syntax was of immense help to me in later years. I had only one grievance about him and that was that he never corrected our weekly essays with a pen. Instead he got each boy to stand up in turn and read his essay aloud. In the second term of my final year the subject of my essay was Catherine the Great, the Empress of Russia. When I had finished reading my essay Father Murphy said to me: 'Read that last sentence again'. I read it, but I must have altered it in some way which he noticed. He asked to see my copy book. The copy book was blank, except for the top right hand of the front page – 'English, Patrick J. Lindsay, 4 September 1927'. I had never written an essay. I had spoken them all and had succeeded in getting away with it until then.

My grievance was that I received a severe caning instead of getting a commendation of some sort. That I did get however, many years later, when I was addressing a political meeting outside the parish church at Lacken where Fr Murphy was then the parish priest. He sent out his housekeeper to invite me to breakfast and apologised for ill-treating me on the day I read out my dissertation on Catherine the Great.

* * * *

I was puzzled by the way in which the teaching of Mathematics was approached. I remember, in my first Mathematics class when we began to learn long division, I felt it was a scandal because, before I had left national school, we had done Arithmetic up to, and including stocks and shares, metric conversion and mensuration. But the teacher was obviously dealing with standards that were generally obtaining at the time – particularly among the day boys from the town. Such could not be said of rural students coming from small two- and three- teacher schools where the teachers covered a very wide course. This was supplemented by my father's assistance; he had a keen interest in Mathematics and English.

In our second year we were taken for Mathematics by the only lay teacher in the school – Joseph Carey from Ennis, the father of Donal Carey now a TD for Fine Gael from Clare. Mr Carey was a brilliant mathematician and wrote beautiful figures with a lovely hand, but he had very little patience with students who tried to make a joke of things. One boy was a particular bane of his life. This boy took no interest in Mathematics or indeed any subject. All he could think about was getting to the sweet-shop and what he could get there.

Mr Carey asked him one day what a cone was and held up the cone for all to see. 'An ice cream tent, Sir' came the reply. Another time he was presented with another kind of figure and when asked what it was he replied: 'The aimsir caite'.

Like so many other colleges in Ireland, St Muredach's was essentially a place for the preliminary training of priests and those who would eventually go to Maynooth. If they were expelled from Maynooth they would find solace in All Hallows in Dublin or St Peters' in Wexford.

The accent was on Classics and we were blessed with two great classics men: Fr Finnerty, who taught Latin with patience, accuracy and perfection, and Fr Cowley who taught Greek with the same attributes.

The 5 years I spent in St Muredach's were happy – although turbulent. We were well fed – hungry perhaps for about a half an hour before the next meal. At any rate nobody died during my time, of starvation or anything else. I must say that in later years the friendships I formed in Ballina were of immense value to me, not alone those who became doctors and whatever but the many who became priests and formed the clerical body of the Diocese of Killala particularly that part of it in North Mayo. They were of great help to me in political campaigns especially in shortening or lengthening sermons according to my requirements.

* * * *

Galway

I went to Galway before career guidance became fashionable. I had received no advice as to what I should do and so I took up Arts with a view to graduating in Classics. I took as my first subjects: Irish, English, Latin, Greek and Logic. Logic I loved, Irish gave me no problem, (I thought), English was quite easy and fascinating by virtue of the fact that we had a wonderful Professor, William A. Byrne, a native of Kildare who always insisted that he could not be sacked because he held the chair by virtue of a Royal Charter, and that it would take the King of England to sack him. He was generally under the influence of drink, as many a good man before him, but his lectures were absolute gems, especially his digressions. One fellow student kept a notebook containing his ramblings on left-hand pages and details of lectures on the right-hand pages.

William Byrne gave me a real interest in the English language. He used to spend Sunday mornings – from 7 o'clock onwards – going from church to church, to listen to the sermons. No matter what condition he would be in from the night before, he would start his Mass round at seven.

On the Mondays he would refer to the sermons he had heard delivered by both the regular and secular clergy (the latter mainly circular), listing all the grammatical mistakes they had made and citing examples as he went along. He said that it was a shame that attention was not paid to sermons during ecclesiastical training.

Galway was a great place in the 1930s. It is still a great place and my favourite city. If I could afford it I would live in Paris, but I would regularly visit Galway. The walkable part of Galway is the most delectable part of any European city that I know.

In my student days the University contained between 500 - 550 students. Everybody knew everybody else. We knew all the Professors in all the faculties; they were a friendly and helpful lot. We had a wonderful dramatic society and, of course, I took a strong interest in politics. During my five years in UCG there was an election every year: a general election in 1933, local elections the next year; a by-election in 1935; another by-election in 1936 and in 1937 I took part in my first General Election in North Mayo, but more about that later.

Public speaking was a great interest of mine. I said earlier that Irish was no problem for me, 'I thought'. The reason for the interjection 'I thought' is that I did not pay that much attention to the texts, reasoning that as a native speaker I would pass my exam without any difficulty. However, I was called into the oral exam before Professor Tomás O'Maille, a gentleman called O'Brien from Queen's University Belfast who was the extern examiner and a gentleman called O'Raghallaigh, or 'Mhici Reilly' as we used to call him. O'Raghallaigh, the father of Padraic O' Raghallaigh of RTE was a great gentleman who started his teaching life in Achill and ended up as a lecturer in Irish at UCG. In the course of the oral, or what the Trinity fellows would call a *viva voce* O'Brien asked me about something or other in a text called *Scealaioct Ceitinn* which had a lot to do with Fionn MacCumhall. My answers were monosyllabic and I displayed total ignorance of the text. But I did understand that at one point he was talking about Fionn MacCumhall. Not being satisfied with my reply, he impatiently asked: 'Cad a tharla dhó sa deire?' With great truthfulness I replied 'Fuair sé bás'. It was not the answer he wanted. With that Professor O'Maille said: 'Amach leat.'

I left. Later I went down to Mhici Reilly who was always approachable and asked if I was in danger. He told me I was – that the Mailleach was very vexed. He looked at me kindly and said: 'Déanai mé mo dhicheall.' And it was not the 'I'll do my best' of the political kind. He did it, and I passed Irish. In the other subjects I got honours.

I gave up Irish and took up Philosophy, Latin and Greek. It was then I encountered my new Professor, Fr Tom Fahy, who became my mentor and close friend. He was of the same political persuasion as I was, and during the weeks before any election campaign I could freely absent myself from lectures. But I paid for it by having to attend his house in the afternoons remaining there sometimes until midnight. As a result I had the benefit of individual tuition from a most urbane yet simple man, a man of great learning, who was able to relate the episodes and historical occurrences of the Classics to the modern times in which we lived.

After Fr Tom Fahy's death in 1973, I was asked by Fr Martin Coen, who was the editor of a periodical in the Galway diocese called *The Mantle*, to write an appreciation. I don't think I can do any better than to reproduce here what I wrote then:

At eighteen, anybody between twenty-five and thirty was old. This view is the subconscious joy or the defective reasoning of youth. At eighteen in the then new Arts building of UCG, one could, for either of these reasons, be forgiven for thinking that Fr Tom Fahy was old. How wrong I was has remained with me a feeling somewhat akin to remorse. Age, of course, has its physical finality; the mind generally is a timeless and ageless mechanism. And here at all times was the real Fr Fahy. He was young, and continued as young as each succeeding set of his students. After a very short time, I was fortunate enough to recognise this fact, and having recognised it, was blessed with the disposition that enabled me to benefit considerably from a situation of respectful and appreciative equality. Added to that, his kindness, tolerance and interest made, what was and continued to be, a wonderful relationship, work. There was an unspoken pride in this mutual craftmanship.

Fr Fahy was a man of great learning, acquired in the main by his perpetual quest for truth. To him things, and, indeed people, were real or they were not. The truth, governing all things, made his adherence to principles of his adoption inflexible. Some people might consider this a fault, but, like the uniform of his joint vocations – teacher and priest – all was black or white: he knew no shades of grey. Of his many great qualities as a teacher, it is difficult to single out one more outstanding than another. I would venture, however, to say that in my experience the one facet that I can never forget was his unfailing facility to sustain one's trust by the use – I think, the deliberate use – of digressions that always contained a significant relevance.

One liked the subject too, not so much because of the power with which it was explained, but rather by the manner in which it was done. And in any assessment of Fr Fahy, one must mention and extend this 'manner' of which I have spoken. Charisma is the modern word. This is a charm or attraction one discovers in oneself and, once discovered, is cultivated and employed in advancing one's career. It is the metier of actors and politicians. To me, it is not good enough to describe accurately the charm of Fr Fahy. I prefer the himeros of which Sophocles spoke in Antigone. This was the charm, simple charm, which is built-in and of which the possessor is quite unconscious. Gowned in his lecture-room; stock ash-stained in his study; riding over the stone walls of his beloved Co. Galway; agile mind keeping time with agile feet after his favourite dog; pulling his chin as a patient listener; in any of these situations this simple charm was the first thing that attracted the attention of even the least observant. Perhaps it was this charm that perennially appealed to the young and kept him young too. In the most unexpected places and passages from Greek or Latin authors he never failed to equate the situations there described with those of our own times. This was his method of instilling patriotism into his pupils. Fr Fahy loved his country. And the only occasion when he appeared to be angry was one that to his mind demonstrated the words or acts tended to impede his country's true progress. In the sense of true progressive, he was the real conservative.

'The cortege to Kiltulla was large and representative. His favourite countryside looked well. The darkness overhead emphasised the solemnity with which his parish received its distinguished son.

I regret that his Requiem Mass was not read in Latin – the language of his discipline and his Church. To him *sursum corda* would have a celestial magnetism; I feel he would have regarded 'lift up your hearts' as little more than exhortation of a coach to his defeated team. I say this through no disrespect, but rather in veneration of my great mentor and friend. Kiltulla churchyard must be beatified by his mortal remains.

Fr Tom Fahy knew that I took a drink and he knew that I occasionally got into trouble at UCG. We were lucky that we had as President for my first two years, a man called Anderson, whom I never saw. He was credited with getting the Marconi invention going before Marconi, though there was never any evidence of that available and such myths are a commonplace at Universities. I was told by a friend, Donal McLoughlin, one of the most brilliant mathematicians I came across as a contemporary, that Anderson was superb. But from our point of view his great quality was that he left us alone.

His successor was a marvellous man called 'Pa' Hynes from the Achonry diocese. He was a great character and a superb student's man. You could be guilty of almost any offence yet he would do his best to help you out, or to hide the offence, or at worst he'd ignore it.

Once in 1935, on a beautiful summer's morning, flying from the flagstaff of the University was the Union Jack – celebrating the Silver Jubilee of King George V. It had been put on the flagpole with thumb tacks and those irate Republicans who were pulling at the ropes trying to get the flag down were making no progress. The flag simply would not budge. Nobody thought about calling the fire brigade and using their ladders – that is until the afternoon. There was a large crowd around the archway. Some were laughing and cheering, others jeering. The 'true' Republicans were foaming from the mouth, beside themselves with anger. Pa Hynes approached me and said: 'Lindsay I am going to ask you who put up that flag, and if you don't tell me, I won't ask anyone else.' I felt the question was an accusation and I said, quite falsely, 'I don't know.' He walked away.

'Pa' had been Registrar before becoming President. He was a great politician if, of doubtful academic status, and his political acumen was exemplified by the fact that he became President against all the odds. On the night he became President he gave us a wonderful evening. We pulled him in a dray from the railway station and pulled the dray all the way to the University and all he could say in his emotion and possibly for some other additional reason was: 'Beidh oíche againn'. We had.

* * * *

I recall one morning being at the postboard in the window of the archway and I saw a card addressed to me. I asked for it and it was handed out to me. It said: 'Please call at your earliest convenience and oblige, J. Hynes.' I knew what it was all about and I walked across the quadrangle for a period which seemed to me to be about 500 years. If it was what I thought it was, it could easily mean rustication. I had had a row at a dance in the Royal Hotel the previous Thursday night in which I got involved with a fellow who was knocking around with a daughter of his housekeeper – a very good looking girl – and things were said which probably shouldn't be said.

I knocked at his door and he said: 'Come in. You're in some trouble. Were you in the Royal Hotel last Thursday night?'

'Yes.'

'Were you drunk?'

'Yes Sir.'

'Do you remember having words with certain people?'

'I do.'

'Very good.'

He then called the girl in question. She came in, I always remember, in a flaming-red dress and she looked even more beautiful than she had on that night.

'This man is here to apologise to you.'

'I beg your pardon Father, I'm not' I said, 'but I'll tell you what I will do. If she apologises for provoking me, I'll apologise for what I said.' She rounded on me, and he said: 'That's enough now, that's good enough, you have apologised, she has apologised, that's enough, it's all over, off you go.' After she left he said: 'Would you care for one?'

'I certainly would.'

'Are you not afraid Fr Tom Fahy will smell it off you?'

'Having got over this hurdle,' I said, 'I'm not afraid of Fr Fahy.'

So he gave me a bumper of good whiskey – in fact he never kept bad whiskey. I went down and Fr Fahy knew all about it, but he never referred to the fact that I was smelling strongly of drink and we went through our full lecture without incident or reference to any trouble.

Now, that was Pa – he was simply great. I remember a day or two before I was leaving UCG I called to him with characteristic cheek, looking for a reference. He pulled out the Union Jack that had been flying two years before and he said to me: 'Tell me now who put that up?'

'Well,' I said, 'there were four of us. I was one of them, but I won't blame the other three.'

He gave me a reference which I have regrettably mislaid but in any event nobody would understand it, because nobody could recognise the upright gentleman that he described in the reference. I got a similar reference from Fr Tom Fahy and armed with these two references I managed to survive.

* * * *

My landlady at that time was a lovely and kind woman who is still living in Galway. I stayed three and a half years in her lodgings after having been put out of my previous digs for eating meat on a Friday.

There was a great relationship in Galway in those days between landladies and students, except for the Salthill landladies who turfed out their tenants on the first day of May to make way for the more lucrative tourists. We shunned Salthill.

* * * *

Through my interests in politics I became friendly with Michael Allen, a solicitor, and a partner of the firm of McDermot & Allen. The McDermot was Hal, a brother of Frank who was in the Dáil as the first leader of the Centre Party, and later a vice-President of Fine Gael though of course he ended up as a nominee of de Valera in the new Senate. I heard recently that Frank never took his Dáil salary and in fact gave it to the St Vincent de Paul in Roscommon, something which didn't make him too popular with his Leinster House colleagues.

Through Michael Allen I got to know Isaac Conroy. He was married to a Welsh lady – hence his granddaughter's name, the celebrated beauty specialist, Bronwyn. I am a great believer in family friendships and in these being extended from generation to generation because, as somebody said: 'You can choose your friends but your relatives are thrust upon you.' I subsequently became friendly with Bronwyn and her sister Virginia Clinton, and am godfather to Bronwyn's elder girl, Sherna. So that's four generations in my span.

Isaac Conroy was one of my great benefactors. He was a man who liked young people, was gregarious, much travelled and a first-class linguist. He was friendly with bohemian types like Augustus John, Charlie Lamb and Francis McNamara, the father-in-law of Dylan Thomas. It was through them that I was introduced to the 'Old Cellar' in Galway. It then had a clay floor, no counter and your whiskey was dispensed by a fellow in a white coat which had never been laundered. But he dispensed great whiskey. I was one of the few students who frequented the place, and as a student I was rarely called upon to pay for my drink. I might have had to give the odd recitation or tell a doubtful story but it was the only currency I had and I used it to very full effect.

One night there was a great carousing in the Old Royal Hotel with Augustus John, Francis McNamara and his current mistress (a beautiful girl from the Midlands), Isaac Conroy and many others. The Royal was owned by a very decent man, John T. Costello, the father of John Costello who owns the Royal Hotel on O'Connell Street in Dublin. As the evening went on and without anyone being aware of it, we transferred from the Royal to the Great Southern Hotel in Eyre Square. Later we left the Great Southern for Francis McNamara's yacht, 'The Mary Anne', berthed down at the docks. Needless to say drinking was continued in each place. At one stage during the night I was roused from my drunken heavy sleep by a roaring from McNamara calling on Conroy and Lindsay to 'get out of my house!' I was never quite certain what the reason was but I think he felt I had been paying too much attention to his young and beautiful mistress – which could have been true. However, I can tell you I had no success.

Since the 'house' happened to be his yacht, getting off wasn't all that easy because we were not in Galway Docks any longer. In a rage, McNamara had earlier ordered his crew to go out to sea and we were somewhere between Black Head and Innisheer. Never will I forget Isaac Conroy's riposte standing in his shirt, socks and suspenders – he was a fat man and fat men don't look attractive in that kind of attire – 'Francis, we would gladly comply with your request, but we are not on the Sea of Galilee.'

We sailed back into Galway the following evening and I was on such friendly terms with Fr Tom Fahy that I didn't have to tell him where I was, or make any excuses.

* * * *

It was while I was at UCG that the movement known as the Blueshirts came into existence. I've said it before and I say it again here, I am an unrepentant Blueshirt.

If it had not been for the presence and support of the Blueshirts, public meetings organised by Cumann na nGaedhael and the Centre Party could not have been held in 1932 and 1933, such was the ferocity of the organised conspiracy against these meetings. The supporters of Fianna Fáil and the IRA, many of the latter just recently released from jail, some of whom had been convicted of very serious offences, set out deliberately and with malice to smash up these meetings, to howl down men like W.T. Cosgrave, Paddy McGilligan and Patrick Hogan who had given the best years of their lives to establishing a strong stable democracy in this country. De Valera, like the Pontius Pilate he could be, made no attempt to stop this happening and, in fact he and his colleagues encouraged the wilder Fianna Fáil supporters and the IRA, to do their damnedest in this regard. The IRA were brazen in their objectives – their slogan 'No free speech for traitors', told it all, since they decided who the traitors were and what punishment was to be meted out to these so called 'traitors'. De Valera as usual hid his real intention behind a statement that it was not the Government's job to make people popular – in other words telling the lads to have a go and nothing would happen them.

All this is fact. It has been documented many times over. But perhaps I could put it at its most simple. We did not start the rows. We defended ourselves, and we provided protection for our people. But the simple fact of the matter is that whereas dozens of Cumann na nGaedhael and Centre Party meetings were broken up or were not allowed take place, dozens of our speakers were attacked, many of their houses were raided and in fact a number of our people died, yet during this period not one Fianna Fáil meeting was interrupted, and not one Fianna Fáil supporter was fatally or even seriously injured. These are facts. My simple question is, where was the aggression coming from? I greatly resent the rewriting of history in such a way as to make the Blueshirts appear to be aggressors.

The Blueshirts were born out of the need for self defence. No less. No more.

As for the charge of facism – that's total nonsense. Most of us did not know what it was and had we known we would have been totally opposed to it. We felt, and indeed we still feel that our democratic credentials were impeccable. We had defended the State, democratically established in the past against all that could be thrown against it during the Civil War and we are not going to change now. As I say, I am and always will be unrepentant in this regard.

I have to say that I do not blame the Guards for the breakup of our meetings. They did their best in very difficult circumstances and as far as I can see dealt fair play all round. Even though I suffered a few clouts from the batons of some of them, I have no doubt I deserved them.

As for Eoin O'Duffy I never regarded him as a man of judgement or a man who could be trusted to stick to his script in a speech. He was a brilliant organiser and a great Commissioner of the Guards and that was where he should have been left but Fianna Fáil sacked him because they did not like or trust him. It was a great mistake to make him leader of Fine Gael – but that's history.

However, the Blueshirt period had its lighter moments too. It was at this time that Eamon de Valera, the then President of the Executive Council was due to visit Galway to unveil a delightful little statue to Sean Phadraic O'Conaire – a man who in truth would have had little enough time for 'Dev'. But some nights beforehand, a few of us climbed over the railings then around Eyre Square, put a blue shirt, a tie, and a beret on Sean Phadraic and replaced the tarpaulin which covered him.

On the following Sunday morning I was going away to address some meeting or other (and where I was generally introduced as 'Professor' even though I was only a student) when a Garda by the name of Gill, originally from Aran, decided to examine the tarpaulin in Eyre Square and ensure that everything underneath was in order. Of course he discovered our plan and took away the element of surprise which was a great pity.

We did have our reward in another way because the platform collapsed with the weight of all the dignatories – dignatories by the way, who would cross the street when Sean Phadraic was alive, in case they would have to buy him a drink.

I saw the same kind of performance at the unveiling of a monument to Sean Phadraic in New Cemetery in Galway a few years ago. But I must exclude from that category of non-buyers of drink, the estimable Dr Sean MacReamoinn, who delivered a splendid address that day.

* * * *

At the formation of the Irish Brigade which General O'Duffy had organised to go and fight on the side of Franco in Spain, O'Duffy offered me a second lieutenantship, which I foolishly and recklessly accepted. But by some means or other a friend of mine approached Fr Tom Fahy to tell him of my intentions.

On that particular morning, which I shall never forget, I was on the docks in Galway at an early hour with several hundred others. It was an atmosphere which is etched in my mind and makes me understand the reasons why people join armies. There were bands, musical instruments, and the singing of 'Faith Of Our Fathers'. But during the course of all this excitement a little Morris two-seater car barged its way onto the quays and out jumped Fr Tom Fahy who said to me: 'What are you doing here?'

'I'm going to Spain'

'You are not, you pup. Stand back there. None of them will fight; they will probably die of dysentry. They will never make any showing. Go back and finish your course of studies.'

I stood back, thoroughly humiliated, when I saw coming along towards the ship a friend of mine, who had spent the previous ten years in Trinity doing Engineering but had emerged with no higher qualification than lightweight boxing champion of Trinity. He had been to Galway for some months in the Engineering school. He was quite a swank. He wore a brown hat, and had a brown crombie coat to match. In fact it was the first crombie coat I ever saw.

He spoke to me and said: 'Are you going to Spain, Pat?'

'No. I've changed my mind.'

'Pity. I'm going to strike a blow for the old Faith.' That comforted me somewhat because I knew that for the past ten years he had not been to church, chapel or meeting house. Anyway, I scuttled back home. The 'Dun Aengus' left with the volunteers, bringing them to a ship out on the high seas and sent them off to Spain.

Time passed and the Irish Brigade came home, having had some losses including Tom Hyde from Kerry, an uncle of Michael O'Leary, later a leader of the Labour Party. One thing I did notice was that my friend of the brown hat and crombie coat had not come back with the Irish Brigade.

Several years elapsed before I met him one day in Grafton Street. We spoke as if time hadn't passed, and naturally for him and for me, the question of having a drink came up fairly quickly. We repaired to Neary's of Chatham Street.

He talked about everything and anything. About coming back to Galway, about getting his degree, about how he was now working with a building company in the North of England. In fact he was prepared to talk about everything except the Irish Brigade and I was extremely anxious to know why he had not come back with them and where he had been, so I put the question straight.

'Oh, I didn't come back. I joined the Spanish Foreign Legion because I wanted to see the thing through to the finish.'

'I see, you were very lucky. You came out of it all without a scratch?' '

'Not really. I got a little dash of V.D. in Barcelona.'

A crusader who had come without his armour! But then at that time, in the Ireland of the 1930s we didn't have an Irish solution to an Irish problem.

* * * *

The O'Conraithe's, or the Conroy's, were a truly remarkable family. Isaac, whom I've mentioned already, was mining in Odessa at the age of nineteen. He was a fluent speaker of Russian, Welsh, English and Irish but to meet him you would never think it. These things are never noticeable in the genuinely humble man. Isaac used to lend me his car in Galway to go to political meetings while the lorries for such meetings were always supplied by the MacDonagh family.

* * * *

Just as I had never met Sean Phadraic O'Conaire, so it was with Michael Conroy. From what Isaac told me, he would appear to have been quite a character in his own right. At one time in the early 1920s he appeared in the Royal Marine Hotel in Dun Laoghaire dressed as a Mohammedan and, to lend weight to the pretence, he was accompanied by four wives all orientally dressed. In those puritanical days, which have not changed a lot, the authorities looked askance at this performance and it eventually reached the attention of the Minister for Home Affairs, Mr Kevin O'Higgins. That minister caused the issuing of a deportation order and in spite of the best representations of the local Galway Cumann na nGaedheal TDs (one of whom, Mairtín Mór MacDonagh was related to him), the bold Michael and his four 'wives' left Dun Laoghaire never to be seen again. The last that was heard of him was that he was fighting on one side or other in the Saarland a few years later.

* * * *

It was while I was still a student at UCG that I had my first experience of teaching, or indeed lecturing. It happened in a somewhat unusual way.

One evening I arrived home for my tea at my digs a little late, not that that was an unusual occurrence. My landlady looked pale, and said: 'Mr. Lindsay, the Dean was here looking for you.' He was always called the Dean even though he had become the President.

I was fully conscious that I had done nothing wrong, certainly nothing that had been found out. The Dean had asked me to be in his office at 8.50 a.m. the following morning. I went there as requested feeling slightly apprehensive.

I walked into his room, breaking three rules. One was that you knocked first; secondly you spoke in Irish; and thirdly you wore a gown.

'Good morning, Lindsay' the Dean said.

'Good morning, Father.'

'I suppose you have no idea what I want you for?'

'No, I haven't.'

'Your friend and mine, Fr Fahy, is not as well as we would like him to be, and he will be absent for some months. It is his wish and, much as it may surprise you, it is my wish too, that you will occupy his Chair in his absence.'

With an eye to the vehicle for pleasure I enquired: 'How much will I get?'

'The standard rate, fifteen shillings an hour.'

It was like winning the Sweep.

'Could I have two pounds on account?' I asked rather cheekily.

The Dean put his hand into his waistcoat pocket, saying: 'Yes, you can, but only on condition that you don't take a drink until you deliver your last lecture today.'

'Alright,' I said, 'I will keep my pledge.'

In those days staff were paid quarterly – or at the end of every term, and they had to stay over a day after term finished in order to get the cheque from the Bursar's office.

In due course I got my first cheque and went down to the Munster & Leinster Bank to draw the funds. I was astounded to be asked: 'How do you want it?' I did not know what he meant and simply replied: 'Anyway at all.'

'Singles, fivers, tenners or twenties?'

'Singles.' I wanted to get a wad of notes and I got them – brand new ones at that!

I headed up to Larry Hynes's pub where I had credit for up to five shillings and that particular day I owed three shillings. I paid him out of the large bundle of notes and had three or four pints. I then went back to my landlady, sat down beside her in the kitchen and asked her: 'How much do I owe you Ma'am?'

'You don't owe me anything except for this week. You paid me for the last week.'

'I don't mean that' I said. 'I mean the little loans from time to time you used to record in your black book. I want to pay you.'

'It'll be soon enough when you're finished, qualified and get a job.'

'Sure I might not pay you at all then.'

So she went and got her little black book and it turned out that I owed her slightly over £30 – a lot of money then. I started counting out notes and had reached to £10 when she sat down. I think she was convinced that I had stolen the money. She knew nothing about my temporary position at the University. I paid her the £30 – she didn't want the extra few pence above that. We are still good friends and I still call to see her in Galway as often as I can.

There was one amusing occurrence during my temporary job. I had overslept one morning and rushed from my digs in Newcastle down to the University for my 9 o'clock lecture. I was about ten minutes late – it was the accepted thing to be that little bit unpunctual.

I donned Fr Fahy's gown and started into Virgil's *Aeneid, Book Two*, translating it and asking questions as I went along. Then I noticed a nun, not a bad looking one either, staring at me but not straight at my face. Her eyes were fixed somewhere in the neighbourhood of my chest. Her stare was so strong and persistent that I put my hand down and discovered I was still in the top of my pyjamas!

* * * *

There were some lovely students at UCG in my time. One was a girl from Kiltimagh called Mary Madden. I was very much in love with Mary, I suppose the kind of love one suffers at that age, sleepless nights wondering if anything will come of it.

We became very friendly and our relationship was recognised as one of the strong lines in the University. At the time I had acquired a new friend who had come from Maynooth, Charlie Durning, a native of Creeslough, Co. Donegal. He did not finish his degree but he was a kind of *fidus achates* to me. In the University magazine one year there was an entry under my name but there was no doubt whatsoever that it was Charlie who had written it. It was as follows:

When Mary looks around for Pat
amidst the archway's loud conclave
From Charlie she elicits that
Her gallant swain's gone home to shave.

Mary now lives in Arklow and we are still in contact. But she created a huge void in my heart during our courtship.

She was one of the first people I knew who went away to France during the summer to learn French. I remember the day she left on the 'Dun Aengus'. The tears were hopping off the flagstones of the Galway docks. I thought I would never see her again. She was going out to join a bigger liner destined for Cherbourg.

I had to be content with waiting from post to post for a letter. It came alright, and my heart sank at the first paragraph.

'Dear Pat', not, 'Dearest Pat', or 'My Darling Pat'. 'I am living with a family in the town of Fougeres, which is built on the remains of an old feudal Castle which is in a marvellous state of preservation.'

The clear message to me from this was that she didn't give a damn about me. How I suffered. I spent a very sleepless night after receiving that letter. We have laughed about it many times since.

* * * *

I have already mentioned that I used to occasionally frequent the pub of Larry Hynes. Larry Hynes was one of the great Galway characters of my time. He was a solid businessman who ran his pub with tremendous precision – no rowdies were ever let in under any circumstances. The pub was situated where the Connacht Laundry can now be found on William Street. There were two entrances, one by an archway into a snug, where only the few were accepted, and the other through an entrance from the street. Larry was always well groomed and always wore a black apron. No matter how young his customers were, all were addressed as 'Mr'. It was a very respectable clientele with a few unusual students thrown in for colour. His regular clients included Gerry Little, a surgeon, Michael Tighe, an engineer and Paddy Kennedy who had just left the civil service to take over the auctioneering firm of Joyce Mackie, Lougheed. Another regular customer and a close friend of Larry's was a decent man from Woodford called Maurice Manning, the Schweppes representative for the West of Ireland, though in truth I never saw him drinking any Schweppes – his tastes were for something slightly stronger. Curiously enough it was with the grandson of that Maurice Manning, of the same name, that I met Dessie Hynes in O'Donoghue's Bar in Dublin for the first time. We were on our way to a lunch in the Unicorn to be hosted by Maurice Manning. Thanks however to the intervention of Dessie Hynes, whom I discovered that day was a nephew of Larry Hynes of Galway, we never actually made it to the lunch in question and I still haven't had it. Dessie Hynes and myself have remained firm friends since that day and I can say truthfully that I know of no publican more decent, more generous and more charitable.

* * * *

While at UCG I took a very active part in the Dramatic Society and we staged several plays. I remember one night playing the country rector in Philpott's play *The Farmer's Wife* in the Columban Hall. Frank Dermody was there and after the performance he came to me and invited me to play 'a silent part' at the Taibhdhearc the following week. 'What's the part?' I enquired.

'Jesus Christ' he said, adding: 'I just want you to wear a long white robe and a crown of thorns. All you'll have to do is pass by a window in silhouette, as if being dragged along by Roman soldiers, pause and look at a girl on the stage, and with that look you are to stop her keeping a date with a Roman officer at his villa.'

The title of the play was *Ag An Am Sin* by Seamus Wilmot, later to become Registrar of the National University, a very decent convivial man. We packed the theatre. Those who knew me and were aware of my fondness for women, thought my part amusing.

I regarded those two particular performances as the greatest advance in dramatic history. I moved from being a country rector to Jesus Christ, all in a matter of days.

* * * *

There were many marvellous characters at UCG in my time. I enjoyed the friendship of a very jovial, hard working medical student named James A. Hughes, known to us all as Jimmy. Jimmy had one suit. It was a plus fours – he didn't own a hat or an overcoat. One day, as I was coming up from the Mall approaching the main bridge, I saw a person coming towards me from the old Central Hospital, now the Regional Hospital. He was wearing an overcoat and a hat but I wasn't certain until I came closer that it was Jimmy. I asked him where he got the hat and the coat and he said: 'B.I.D.' – it was the first time I had heard these initials and I asked him what they meant. He said: 'Brought In Dead' – he had got them from a corpse.

In fact I now know the identity of the person from whom the overcoat and the hat (incidentally both of excellent Connemara tweed – and matching) were taken. It was a man who had drowned in the Corrib. He came from a wealthy family in West Galway and they could well afford to lose his coat and hat in that way. I'm sure they would not have begrudged it to Jimmy, and the family are still thriving and wealthy.

In addition to his many lovable qualities, Jimmy was a superb musician, both as a singer and a violinist. I remember the two of us were brought before a Disciplinary Committee on one occasion for singing a Requiem Mass in the back yard of Paddy Lydon's public house in Eyre Street. We had been singing for some time, Jimmy, Donal McLoughlin and myself. Donal had passed out in the middle of his third song which he invariably started but never finished. His three great songs were, 'The Boys of County Mayo', 'The Stone Outside Dan Murphy's Door' and the third was 'The Bould Phelin Brady, The Bard of Armagh' and he invariably passed out during this third song. After he passed out Jimmy sang the Requiem and such was the quality of his voice and the slightly bizarre nature of the offering at that hour that a crowd quickly gathered. When we were brought before the Disciplinary Committee we were simply reprimanded. What we had done was no crime of any kind.

Jimmy's singing was to be of great advantage to us when, as members of the Officers Training Corps we made our first visit to Finner Camp.

We arrived on the Saturday, with our buttons fully polished, our Sam Brown belts, our epaulettes, the lot – prospective officers and doubtful gentlemen. We made for Bundoran with our last shilling, having paid sixpence each for a taxi. We were sauntering along the footpath in Bundoran hoping to meet somebody we knew, which was a somewhat forlorn hope, as we were far from home. But as luck would have it, I did see an old teacher of mine from primary school. I went up and spoke to him and being in uniform he wasn't quite certain who we were. Eventually, he recognised us and asked us the meaning of the garb. We told him and to my alarm and surprise he didn't ask us to have a drink. The secret however, of his somewhat strange behaviour, was that he was returning from Lough Derg and was still fasting. However, we invited him to come and have a drink with us, and when the two pints of Guinness for us and the mineral water for him arrived, Hughes and I were engaged in such an animated conversation, that he was obliged to pay. After some time, when he was about to leave, I followed him and managed to get a ten shilling note from him. We went back and sat at our table. We had already removed our military caps and were beginning to ease the neck bands of our tunics by unfastening the clasps.

We were in a hotel called The Palace Hotel, owned by a lovely family called Conlon, and their three daughters if not four, formed a band in the lounge. One played the piano, the other played the guitar, the other the cello and the fourth, Mary, who was later killed in an air raid in London, played the violin. After some little time, Hughes went up, stood in front of Mary Conlon, bowed, and asked her for the violin. She gave it to him. He played as nobody had ever played before in the Palace Hotel, or, I believe since. His success culminated in our getting our names on to the visitors book, and, what was more important, we were now in a position to get credit, which was no mean achievement on our first afternoon in Bundoran.

Our enthusiasm carried us a little bit too far. That night we walked down the streets of Bundoran, caps in hand, tunics slung over our shoulders, Sam Brown belts God knows where. By this stage we had been joined by Raymond Cross, long since dead, but a man who was the uncle of Kevin Cross, later to marry my daughter Alison. Raymond was a cadet corporal. We went into Carrolls which was a hotel-cum-dancehall. When the bouncer refused us admission, Hughes dealt with that situation by rendering the bouncer somewhat stunned, if not worse and we went upstairs and into a room which we knew was a drinking room by reason of signs on the stairs – 'Private Lounge'. Coming into the room I never saw more gold braid in all my life than on the caps which were on the table, which was also amply covered by full bottles of whiskey, brandy and anything else.

Our own commanding officer, Lt Mulcahy from Galway, who was married to a daughter of a medical professor named Tommy Walsh, said to us in Irish: 'In ainm De, bí ag imeacht.'

We didn't go, and eventually the man who seemed to have more gold braid than the rest of them stood up and said: 'Get Out'.

Jimmy Hughes said: 'Who are you?'

'I'm Major General McSweeney, Assistant Chief of Staff.'

'Well,' said Hughes, 'I'm James A. Hughes, cadet OTC, number 1411 and make what you like about it.'

He pulled out a chair, sat down and poured himself a glass of whiskey, whereupon we all followed suit.

Nothing more happened that evening and such was our boldness and presumption, fuelled no doubt by the substantial amount of alcohol we had imbibed, that we insisted on going back with the officers in their cars to Finner. They however, had the last word. They didn't allow us in the officers' gate. We had to go to the other gate where of course we were late and as a result we were court-martialled the following morning.

The court-martial was a most imposing ceremony, especially seeing a non-commissioned officer coming along with a pair of rusty scissors, removing the Corporal's stripes from Raymond Cross's sleeves. Hughes and myself had nothing to lose. We were rankers already, but we were detained and confined to barracks for the rest of our period there. However it was enjoyable because we were regarded as heroes by the NCO's and privates who were there already, and we were entertained in their messes. In fact we had a marvellous time, all for free. Jimmy later qualified in medicine. He spent a short time in West Limerick in Ardagh, but didn't like it very much and went to Canada. He died in Florida two years ago.

There was another great character at UCG named Jack Mullarkey who came from Tubbercurry, Co. Sligo. Jack graduated in the mid 1930s and he was in the same position as all of us were then – no job, no prospects and no chance of getting into the Guards unless you were a card-carrying member of Fianna Fáil. One area which was quite popular with a few people in those days was to seek a job in the Palestine Police.

Jack applied, and according to himself he had six or seven aunts all doing Novenas, hoping he would not get in because they feared he might be killed. He went to London for an interview and when he faced the interview board he saw that the man on his right-hand side facing him had an empty right-hand sleeve, the fellow in the middle had a patch over his eye, and the third fellow had a straight leg which meant it was artificial. This had a fairly salutary effect on Jack, who saw at once some of the risks attendant upon service in the Palestinian Police. In any event he had little chance of getting this job because as soon as he gave his name as 'Mullarkey' one of the interview board said: 'Don't tell me you come from ***** Tubbercurry?'

The gentleman in question had served with the Black and Tans in the Tubbercurry area and clearly he remembered the Mullarkey name and had no great opinion of them. So Jack reckoned that it was the conduct of the Mullarkey's in the Black and Tan times rather than the Novenas of his aunts which prevented him getting into the Palestine Police.

* * * *

In addition to doing my Masters degree in Classics I also got a H.Dip in Ed at UCG – though it was a course and qualification for which I had little or no respect.

The H. Dip in my time was divided into four parts – the history, the method, the organisation and the psychology of education. It could have been reduced to four simple sentences:

The history of education was the hedge school.

Method – always use a black board.

Organisation – Never build a school near an open sewer or dung heap.

Psychology – Get a boy or a girl out of the classroom before he or she wets the floor.

Years later I met Seamus Wilmot, at this stage the NUI Registrar. He said: 'By the way Pat, there is an unconferred Higher Diploma in Education in my office. Would you do something about it?'

I replied; 'If you know anybody to whom it might be of use, give it to him or her.'

* * * *

I left Galway, seen off by a large group of friends outside the Great Southern Hotel, in October 1937. It was in the good old days when we had a multiplicity of railways. While waiting in Athenry for the Ballina train I had a few drinks... and a few more ... and a few more.

Later I forgot to cross the platform for the Ballina train so I got on to a train going to Galway, where, when I arrived, I found my friends still in the bar at the Great Southern.

I stayed another couple of days before eventually going home. My luggage however had gone on and it was later found in St Johnstone, in Co. Donegal.

It was, I felt, not an inappropriate way to end five of the best years of my life.

* * * *

Cavan to Dublin

Inow spent a year without paid employment. The only serious job offer was in Khartoum, which on my father's advice I rejected. However at the end of this idle, sometimes reckless, most times feckless year I got a telegram: 'Can you accept Classics Mastership at Royal School Cavan? Ring Cavan 65. Headmaster.'

I had to cycle 15 or 16 miles to the nearest telephone but to my great delight the Headmaster and I arranged everything over that phone.

On my arrival in Cavan I was met by a man named Freddy Hall who taught Maths. On the journey from the bus stop to the school he gave me a mournful tale of the misfortunes attached to becoming a secondary school teacher.

I did not care, nor could I care less; it was just great to get something.

I was received by the Headmaster and his wife and that night I had dinner with them for the first and last time. During the dinner they were X-raying me – not on academic matters but on social matters and manners. They asked me if I had ever ridden with the Galway Blazers. I said I had. This was not fully a lie because I had driven Fr Tom Fahy's car from Athenry to Loughrea while he rode with the Blazers.

My answer had very nearly disastrous consequences for me! I did not know that they had a riding school at Cavan Royal and I had not been on anything four legged other than an ass before. Later the Headmaster's son told me he had a horse called 'Dapple' saddled for me. 'Dapple' appeared to me to be bigger than the horse of Troy.

How was I going to mount the horse? Luckily he told me: 'There is a mounting block over beside her.' I did not know what a mounting block was, but I saw this butt of a tree and concluded correctly that this was the item referred to. So I got into the saddle, feeling rather like Tom Mix, and I was only sorry that nobody was looking. I eventually got into a trot and then a canter. After that triumph I did a lot of riding on that old horse. It is the best cure after a bad night. A good early morning gallop takes some beating.

During that one and only dinner with the Headmaster and his wife I was told that there were three services the following morning: Church of Ireland, Presbyterian and Methodist, all at 11.30 a.m. 'I am a Papist,' I said, asking 'what time is the last Mass?'

The blood drained from their faces. How could a man with a name like Lindsay be a Catholic? The headmaster said nothing, but he was deeply shocked. This was the Ireland of the 1930s. Religious bigotry was an everyday fact of life and a small number of people, on learning I was a Catholic, treated me almost as if I were a leper. But this was not true of the students nor indeed of any of my colleagues.

The Royal School was a co-educational establishment and I must say I still regard it as a great privilege to have had that experience, and, having had it, I understand less and less the conditions of the present day, especially the insistence from so many quarters, of religious or sexual segregation. I think that if there was more freedom for boys and girls to mix and for different religions to intermingle we would have a better country. I was the only person in Cavan Royal carrying the banners of Rome, tattered maybe, but flying, and there was never one word of discrimination or bigotry between me and my fellow teachers.

* * * *

One day, I was teaching *De Senectute* in class. One section describes how the souls of the dead now being on Mount Olympus with the gods are able to intercede for friends on earth. A girl called Mildred Strong said with obvious impishness: 'Mr Lindsay, isn't that like your idea of the Saints?'

'Well yes' I said and, just as I uttered the words, my eye caught another girl called Betty Coffey from Bawnboy Co. Cavan, the daughter of a Fine Gael county councillor.

'I'll put it this way' I said. 'If the people of Bawnboy have some kind of grievance, or some good suggestion, they don't all come in convoy to the County Council. They go and see Betty Coffey's father and put their case to him. He then goes to see the County Secretary. In that way our Saints resemble County Councillors and TD's – intermediaries who would intercede on their behalf.'

Later I told this story to Dr O'Boyle when he was Bishop of Killala. His reply was: 'Well, I am sure your pupils thought an awful lot less of the Saints after that.'

* * * *

When I came to Dublin in 1940 after teaching in the Royal School in Cavan for two years, I arrived at O'Connell Bridge with three shillings and six pence to my name. I left Cavan leaving a debt of ten shillings in Phil Galligan's pub in Bridge Street, which I later paid.

I had friends in 105 Lower Baggot Street, a family named Fallon who had originally come from Athenry. I used to visit them during trips to the Fine Gael Ard Fheis in my student days in Galway, usually along with a chap called Paddy Cawley from Craughwell, a relation of the Fallons. He later became a TD for one term. Having tried very hard to get into the Dáil, he tried even harder to get put out.

I felt I had an entree to the Fallon household – which was also a biggish boarding house – and so I walked there from the bus stop opposite McBirney's with my meagrely filled fibre suitcase. Mary Fallon, who was a few years older than me and a fine looking girl, opened the door and greeted me effusively. I asked her if she could give me a bed for a week until I found accommodation and a job. 'The fact that you have no job makes not the slightest difference' she said.

'You are perfectly welcome to come here for breakfast, lunch and tea Pat, but you are not staying.'

Obviously Cawley and I had blotted our copy books in some way during our earlier visit. I asked her if I could leave my case in the hall and she replied: 'Of course'. Then I went across the street to Larry Murphy's pub. Here I met Eugene O'Donoghue, who then worked in the Estate Duty Office. I asked him if there were any spare beds over in 105 and he said that I could share his room because there had been no one in it for the previous three months.

I was seventeen weeks there before the Fallons found out. I never paid a shilling but then, I hadn't it to pay. I used to give grinds, and I got some work in vocational schools through the late Martin Gleeson, then a great friend of Liam Burke, the General Secretary of Fine Gael, and once a teacher himself in Castleknock.

In the course of the grinds I came across a few of my former pupils from Cavan Royal; they were studying Divinity at Trinity. They asked me if I would coach them in Biblical Greek. I said: 'Which text do you want?' 'The Acts of the Apostles' came the reply. 'Have any of you got them?' They hadn't. As it happened, I was a frequenter of Greene's Library above the bookshop in Clare Street. There was, and is, a post-office there, where in those days one applied for the keys to the Classics' room. You got it only if you were known. It contained almost everything that had ever been written in Latin or Greek – some new, and some secondhand. The search for what you were looking for was difficult because the index was poor. Besides, scholars who came there often left the place in a mess because once they had found what they wanted they would rarely put the books back in their proper place.

One had to climb a ladder to the top shelves – but generally the text books were low down on the floor. I was down on my hunkers and I had just come across 'The Acts of the Apostles' in Greek. I was delighted but my delight was short-lived because my back was nearly broken by a whole clatter of Aristotle's *Poetics*, which are heavy volumes that were falling from the top shelves on to me.

I managed to get up and straighten myself. Then I looked up at a little man on top of the ladder and addressed him vigorously and impolitely.

'I am dreadfully sorry' he said coming down the ladder. 'Are you a classical scholar?'

'No,' I said, 'I'm only leaning towards it.'

'Well, you've damn fine language.'

'Who are you?'

'My name is Alton. I'm the Provost of Trinity.'

We retired to a nearby cafe and had a great chat. He was a charming man who lived in Northbrook Road in Ranelagh. We became good friends and I went there to see him afterwards.

As a result of that rather unclassical first meeting, I went down to Trinity the following Saturday, and solemnly in Latin, was sworn in as a reader of the library and given a card which I still have, though I have to say I never put it to any great use.

It was at this time that Michael Tierney, a former Cumann na nGaedhael TD for North Mayo, and the then Professor of Classics at UCD and later to become President of that institution, began to take a friendly interest in me. He knew of my background in Classics and of my Mayo origins (in fact my father had campaigned for him in many elections) and my Fine Gael leanings and at this stage he prompted me to do a Ph. D. in Classics. The title of my thesis was '*De Mortibus Persecutorium*' by an early Christian author called Lactantius. The subject matter was fairly gruesome. It dealt with the awful deaths of some of the Emperors who had persecuted Christians in early Rome. I would say I got almost five sixths of the work done, mainly in longhand. I carried it around with me religiously, but one night I left it behind in a pub. I could never remember which pub it was and in spite of a thorough search I never recovered it and so could never complete my Doctorate.

It was also at this time that Michael Tierney arranged for me to edit some Browne and Nolan texts – mainly Virgil – for a fee of 100 guineas. I have never forgotten his generosity at this most penurious time.

In later years I felt greatly consoled when I heard James Dillon say with a little scorn when he became Minister for Agriculture: 'My God, I am the only person in my Department who is not a doctor of something or other.' When I look at some of the honorary doctorates today and the way in which they are given out so cheaply by some of the universities I have no regrets at all.

* * * *

In the course of my teaching career I taught in seventeen schools in Dublin in three and a half years. The shortest stay was half an hour in Ross's on St Stephen's Green. It was a beautiful day and I came out after the 10 o'clock break and never went back.

I taught at Belvedere College for three weeks. I did not like the regimentation there; they said the 'Hail Mary' at the beginning of every class, so I left. I taught in Ringsend and at the Comhairle Le Leas Oige in Gt Denmark Street and in Mount Street.

It was at that point that I had a real stroke of good fortune. Herbert Foster, a former student from Cavan Royal, later to become agricultural attaché at the Irish Embassy in London, a wonderful friend, phoned me to tell me that he had got a 'school' to Trinity which meant he was giving up his teaching job at Sandford Park. My first reaction was to say to Herbert: 'Foster, I always knew you were dull enough to be good at exams.'

However, the point of his call was to tell me he would recommend me for his job at Sandford Park. He told me to go to Sandford Park, that the headmaster, Mr Cordner would not interview me, but that, if I wished I could interview him, and he assured me that the job was mine. He was as good as his word. Herbert's brother, Ernest Foster, had been a colleague of mine at Cavan Royal before becoming headmaster at Waterpark in Waterford. Ernest's son, Roy Foster is now a distinguished historian.

Mr Cordner was a gentleman who played cricket for Ireland and Canada. One of my jobs at Sandford Park was to say 'Grace' but this was one of the many jobs that I delegated and I used to get the prefects to say it for me. This greatly displeased the matron, a Miss Gillespie, who could not have been regarded as being well disposed to the Great Communion of Rome. She told the Headmaster that I wasn't saying Grace. He very politely suggested that I might say Grace once or twice to smooth the Matrons' feathers.

When I came down the next morning I hit the side of a glass with a spoon and intoned the Grace in the Catholic form, just like a Jesuit. Miss Gillespie was standing with a pot of porridge at the end of the refectory. I never said Grace there again, nor was I ever asked.

Sandford Park was a great school. Classes numbered no more than twelve. All denominations were taught there – Catholics, all the various Protestant sects and Jews. It was a haven for the children of parents who were not keen on religion and it had been set up in 1922 as a place for people who thought the end of the world had arrived, now that Whitehall was no longer in control. It was a bit like the Law Library and also a bit like Caesar's Gaul divided into three parts Catholics, Protestants and Catholics who wished they had been born Protestant.

The school was tolerant and open. You did not know what anyone's religion was and you didn't ask. I came down one morning with a particularly bad head and ran into a boy called Harry Jackson kicking a half-pumped rugby ball against the pictures in the hall – or maybe he was kicking the ball against the wall and sometimes hitting a picture. 'Jackson' I said, 'What are you doing?'

'Nothing Sir' he replied in typically boyish fashion.

'One hundred lines Jackson.'

'But Sir...,' 'Jackson, two hundred lines, and by the way, why aren't you at Rev. Austin Carrie's scripture class?'
'But Sir...', 'Jackson, one thousand lines.' I finished up somewhere around fifteen thousand lines. Jackson just shrugged his shoulders. He knew I did not care if he did not write one line.

A colleague called Auchmuty who taught History, (later he became Professor of History at the University of Alexandria) came along and said: 'Lindsay, it's bad enough for you to be on the staff of an heretic institution such as this, but giving one of your own brethren fifteen thousand lines for not attending a Church of Ireland scripture class is going too far.'

* * * *

These were the war-time years and neutrality as it was practiced in Ireland was fairly undefinable and certainly undefineable in the way it was applied. Certain of the combatants having been captured, remained here all the time. Some others were given a free run across the border or put onto Irish ships and left off at the nearest appropriate island, which happened to be Britain.

I recall one evening, it was I think in 1945. There was at the time in Ballsbridge in the RDS grounds a thing called a military tattoo. That tattoo had been visited by a young American naval man who happened to be a nephew of Thomas O'Toole a friend from Mayo who was in the customs and excise in Dublin. Thomas was entertaining this young American in the Gresham Hotel and he asked me to come along and, as I was always quick to accept an invitation which included a free meal and a free drink, I went along with great enthusiasm. We took our places at the table of the old Grill Room at the Gresham and sitting in the corner on his own was an American army chaplin – of what persuasion you wouldn't know because all the Christian denominations simply wore a cross on the lapel of the tunic.

So I said to the naval chap that he should ask his confrère from America to join us. He said: 'Well, we don't speak to the army much, but I will.' He brought him over and he just stood there and said: 'My name is Phil Sweeney, Sacred Heart Order, South Chicago.'

We all acknowledged the introduction, and gave our names, and invited him to sit, which he did. He told us he had come off the boat earlier that afternoon from Holyhead and that he was staying in a rooming house in Hatch Street, and was having a look around prior to his departure for Mayo the following day to visit his relatives.

Now hearing Co. Mayo, and all of us coming from there, we were naturally interested and enquired what part. He said Ballina. Now there were two distinct families of Sweeney in Ballina known to me and it was very important to place him with the correct one. After a few enquiries he said: 'Well, there are two smaller names in the address – Doohoma and Mount Jubilee.' I took a hard look at him and asked: 'Have you cousins named Kennedy?' He said; 'Yes' and I said, 'I went to school with your first cousin, Francis Kennedy' and then of course we became bosom friends.

Shortly afterwards Tom O'Toole and his nephew left us and the first question Sweeney put to me after they left was: 'What do you do in this town when "the bad law" begins to operate?' I said: 'I don't quite follow what you mean by "the bad law".'

'Well, your pubs close at 10 o'clock. What do you do then?' So I outlined to him various measures which could be taken – go to a friendly pub that wasn't too finnicky about the hours they kept, but I said I wouldn't advise that because you might get into rough company and after all, you are in a Padre's uniform. Or, I said, you could go to a club, if you know somebody who is a member of a club – I wasn't – or you could find out where there was a party and take along a little drink and join up.

He said: 'Have you no cabaret – no dancing girls – no night clubs?'

I said: 'No, we are a very holy country.'

He said: 'Holy bedamned – no night clubs, no dancing girls – no wonder you're neutral – you've nothing to fight for.' (Later, when I told that story to James Dillon – like Queen Victoria – he was not amused).

We went across to the Catholic Commercial Club, now gone, and we got in there and of course he became a curiosity straight away. We were treated with great hospitality by the members, such members as were there, and the question of our neutrality came up and he said: 'Well, you had a row with the British lasting seven hundred years – that was some row – I don't blame you for not coming to their assistance.' Then he said: 'Your kith and kin, that's me, the Americans asked you for the use of your ports and you refused – we feel pretty sore about that, but it's all over now. We won, it doesn't matter. But you really missed your chance when the Japanese raped four of your nuns in the Far East – that was your chance to declare war on Japan. You were at a safe distance and you were totally safe. You would today be on the boat to the Peace Conference. You would be steerage, but at least you would be on it!'

The following day he left and I was not to see him again. However he arrived down in my part of the parish where his father and mother had come from. His visit coincided with a visit to the parish, by the late great boxing star, Jack Doyle and his movie star girlfriend Movita. They went to the 'banqueting hall' of Johnny McGeehan to which I have already referred and somehow, in a village of three pubs it wasn't very long before my father got together with Fr Phil Sweeney, Jack Doyle and Movita. It was some gathering in a small village and certainly the carry-on would hardly have been regarded as edifying by our very conservative neighbours.

In fact, Phil Sweeney, had considerable difficulty, as a result of this camaraderie, in getting permission from the local priest to say Mass. The priest had a doubt as to whether he was actually a priest at all or not. But eventually he did, through the intervention of my father who explained who he was and to whom he was related. Having read Mass, he turned around to address the people. He told them how delighted he was to be in the church where his father's and mother's baby brows were laved in the water of Baptism. He thanked them for their hospitality and the wonderful welcome they had given him in the course of the previous week but that it didn't surprise him since 'he was only two hours in Dublin when he met a typical, Christian Son of the Parish – Pat Lindsay.' Now the remarkable thing was that the people's respect for the priest prevented anybody leaving at the mention of my name. Otherwise I think some might have.

* * * *

Moya

At a very early stage during my sojourn in Cavan, I met a most remarkable woman, Mrs John Brady of 25/26 Main Street, who with her husband ran an extensive drapery and footwear business. Curiously enough I met her first at a Knights of Columbanus dinner, at which I was made to feel extremely uncomfortable because several of the people there refused to accept my right to attend. Having met Mrs Brady I discovered that she too was a native of Co. Mayo. She was a Catherine Fahy from a little village called Lavallyroe outside Ballyhaunis. She had remarkable qualities; she was a great businesswoman, she was charitable, she took tremendous interest in the affairs of the town, especially in the Jubilee Nurses Committee.

We became exceptionally good friends and I enjoyed the freedom of her very hospitable home. I got to know all the members of her family, with the exception of one daughter who was away in Dublin doing a secretarial course, having finished her education at the Dominican Convent in Cabra.

I left Cavan in 1940, and during my precarious financial existence in Dublin in the ensuing years I occasionally saw a friend from my own parish, Paddy Holmes. We met one day in a pub near Amiens Street and, quite uncharacteristically, we were both in possession of a certain amount of money. That money was not destined for a thrift account in a bank or post-office, so we set off to visit some pubs. Eventually we found ourselves in a pub at the back of the Four Courts but, not knowing the owner or the staff, we had to leave at the beginning of the 'Holy hour' at 2.30 p.m. Coming out to the street we saw almost in front of us what looked like a Protestant church, but was in fact St Michans. We read the notice outside about visitors being welcome to go down to the vaults.

Having nothing better to do to while away the hour until the pub opened again we visited the vaults. The curator showed us the bodies of the Sheares brothers and the body of a nun in a great state of leathery preservation. As we were passing these remains the Curator said: 'This is the body of a crusader. They say it's luck to shake hands with him.' We shook hands whole-heartedly with the crusader and left. We wound our way across the Liffey, visiting various pubs on our route, and finally reached what was then Kelly's of Upper Leeson Street, now the Leeson Lounge. It has in fact been much extended since then and has taken in a grocery shop owned by the Caldwells who lived at number 26 and whose friendship I enjoyed. I used their credit for a good portion of each month and was on warm terms with Mrs Caldwell, who herself took an occasional drink in Kelly's snug.

Paddy and I were halfway down a pair of pints when it became obvious that the money we had left would not bring us to the time that is immortalised by some scribe who wrote: 'The saddest words of tongue or pen are, "now gents, please, it's ten past ten".'

I got an idea, I went over to Mrs Caldwell and asked her if she knew of two girls who might be staying in a flat in Upper Leeson Street and who might be customers. One, I explained would have a pronounced northern accent and her name was Rita Macken from Enniskillen. The other was the one member of the Brady family that I had never met.

'I am not sure, but what do they look like?'

'I don't know, I never saw them.'

'Well' she said, 'there are two girls, and one of them certainly has a northern accent, in the flat next door in No. 27.

I returned to Holmes and told him to mind my drink. I mounted the steps of No. 27, lit a match and there were the magic words opposite the bell, 'Brady and Macken'.

I pressed the bell and after some little time the door was opened by Rita Macken who obviously did not like the look of me. I asked her if

Miss Brady was in and she said: 'Who shall I say?'

'A friend of her mothers.'

She went back upstairs and a rather petite girl wearing glasses came to the door and said: 'Hello' rather diffidently.

'I am a friend of your mothers. My name is Pat Lindsay.'

'Oh yes, I've heard of you.'

'I won't delay you now,' I said apologetically, 'but could you lend me a pound?'

'Yes' she said, and she went upstairs and extracted a pound note from what I later discovered was a little black box where she kept her treasured possessions, returned and handed it to me. I then departed. My one regret was that she was so nice and polite in respect of my request, that I hadn't asked her for a fiver.

Back in Kelly's I put the pound note down on the counter and proceeded to order two more pints. Some minutes later as we raised the two fresh pints to our lips Paddy Holmes aptly remarked: 'Who said it was lucky to shake hands with the Crusader?'

In the following weeks I felt that I should do something about giving back the borrowed pound. I thought it might be a good idea to call round to Moya's flat and invite her to the pictures. This I did one bright summer's evening. I was wearing what I would say was the first genuine 'bainin' in Dublin. I used to call it my seamless garment because it did not have seams – the sleeves had just been stuck on by the Connemara makers. I was also wearing sandals without socks.

Moya politely refused to accompany me to the pictures dressed as I was, and in hindsight she was right. I told her I would call again when I had managed to get my suit in good condition.

Eventually we managed to go out to the pictures and a friendship developed. My behaviour did not command her highest respect, and she was right. I really was no great addition to anyone. So, after a very long period of great patience on her part she finally dismissed me from her life.

The shock wasn't great. In my arrogance I reasoned that Moya wasn't the only pebble on the beach and so I treated the matter casually. She left Dublin somewhat later to help in the family business, where she displayed all of her mother's qualities.

I did not see her again until 21 April 1944 when I went to Cavan to attend her father's funeral. My apparel was not dignified or respectable, but through the good offices of her brother, Tom, I was able to borrow a pair of shoes and an overcoat out of the shop. Moya was highly indignant and never spoke to me. My offence was further compounded by the fact that I walked with her four brothers for three miles from Cavan to Killegary graveyard. All I succeeded in getting from that outward display of devotion were blisters from the new footwear.

Eventually, I was called to the Bar in November 1946 and soon afterwards got an attack of alopecia and lost all my hair. When Moya was told this she commented: 'Well, God has got even with that fellow.'

In late 1951 I was returning to Dublin from a sitting of Sligo Circuit Court. As was my custom, I used to vary my route to avoid the boredom of the same roads, the same bends and the same towns. This day I decided to take the road through Leitrim to Carrick-on-Shannon and Longford, rather than go across the Curlews and into Boyle. As I was coming into the village of Ballyfarnon I noticed that there was a sharp left-hand turn across the bridge. I applied the brakes, but they failed. By sheer luck I missed the bridge and wasn't injured. When I went to a local garage I was told my car had no brake fluid. It would take at least an hour to have the car fixed.

I walked up and down the street because I wasn't drinking at the time and there was little for me to do. At the post-office I noticed the word Ballyfarnan and it brought my memories back to my first journey from home to Cavan Royal. Despite my various philanderings – and they were both various and disreputable – Moya's memory had never left me.

Boldly, I went into the phone booth in the post-office and phoned Cavan 93. Mrs Brady answered the phone and I asked for Moya. When she came on the phone she said: 'Is it you?'. 'Yes,' I said, 'I'm in Ballyfarnan getting some repairs to my car. If I go around by Cavan, will you give me a meal?'

'I will' she answered, 'but you won't get any meat because it's Friday.'

So I went to Cavan that night and left the following Monday. Our romance was once again alive, the rest of our courtship was happy and uneventful. Preparations were made for marriage though I disappointed Moya by standing in the by-election in North Mayo in 1952 which I lost but which resulted in my ignoring Moya for a considerable period.

Then came the question of an engagement ring. That almost ended in disaster as I was delayed in Galway – my own fault almost certainly – and only arrived back in Cavan the day we were to go to Dublin for the ring. I tried to arrange 'protection' for myself by bringing Judge Durkan's crier with me. It did not work.

I got a very sharp welcome from Moya: 'You don't appear to be perturbed, or disturbed, or interested in this wedding. Do you want to go ahead with it?'

'Of course I do, and I shall look appropriately green at the right time.'

We went to Dublin to get our engagement ring but with my usual lack of organisation, I had not bothered to book a room in the Gresham, even though I had arranged for a jeweller to come there so that a ring could be chosen. I spoke to Toddy O'Sullivan, the Manager but he hadn't a room to offer us so he suggested the ante room of the Ladies. The jeweller arrived and we repaired inside. He opened his box with an assortment of rings, while I watched, trembling, with my mind racing from price to bank manager.

Moya chose well, and she chose reasonably. I put the ring on her finger and we went downstairs and had a meal.

We had arranged to get married on 3 September 1952 and the reception was to be held in the Park Hotel, Virginia, Co. Cavan. However, we then discovered that the local Agricultural Society was holding its Annual Bull Show in Virginia on the same day! So, not being anxious to share with that bovine congregation we decided to postpone the wedding until later on that month.

We were married in the Cathedral in Cavan. My best man was James P. Trainor and the bridesmaid was Rita Macken, Moya's former flatmate. As we were kneeling side by side at the altar, Trainor said to me: 'I'm feeling sick.' 'I think you should go to the sacristy,' I said. 'Get sick if you can and return carrying some class of prayer book or missal.'

Before the wedding breakfast, I had gone through the telegrams specifically to see if any should not be read out. Only one was removed. It was addressed to Mrs Moya Lindsay, Park Hotel, Virginia, Co. Cavan and the message was: 'Galway is grateful to you, Madam.' It was signed Jack Deasy, a friend of mine, who wanted to embarrass me but I was too quick for him.

Before the wedding ceremony I wrote a little note on that telegram and passed it to Moya just after she had entered that Cathedral: 'You look lovely. Do I look appropriately green?'

We honeymooned in Scotland, a marvellous experience, and it was there on the Isle of Skye that I learned from another solicitor the meaning of the word 'vacancies' in windows. In other words I had entered the Bed & Breakfast scene.

I wasn't short of money but I might have been, if Moya's mother had not handed me an envelope quietly before we left. It contained £300, a lot of money in the early 1950s. The notes were the old white English fivers and I used to extract the required amount in the men's toilet prior to paying any bill.

Typically in my case we had no home. I had made no preparations. I was in lodgings in Sandymount 'living with a poets widow' – a charming woman who was slightly fond of the drink which meant that on somedays you might not get an evening meal. Eventually I set about looking at suitable houses so that they could later be vetted by Moya and her mother. They broke my heart, I used to refer to the two of them as the Court of Appeal. They would travel up from Cavan, look at the houses I had picked out and reject them one after the other. This went on for months. I remember one particular house – a bungalow in Sandyford, overlooking the city, and I was certain that it would meet with their approval. We drove out there and as we were standing outside, I said: 'Look at that view of Dublin Bay and Howth beyond. Isn't it beautiful? That view alone is worth thousands.'

'I suppose it is' answered Moya, 'but when would you see it? By moonlight?'

We eventually selected and bought number 17, The Rise, Mount Merrion. It was a gift from Mrs Brady to us. This meant that we started married life in our own home, relieved of the obligation of a mortgage, and for that I have always been very grateful to my mother-in-law – though for much more as well.

Moya and I had a great life together – somewhat more than 25 years. We celebrated our silver wedding anniversary in September 1977 and it was on our return from our cottage in Annaghvaan in Connemara, that Moya died suddenly in the forecourt of Orwell Motors in Rathgar. I'm not certain that she died there, but she was certainly dead on admission to hospital.

My daughter Alison was with me at the time. She had come to meet us because my car wasn't going well. We followed the ambulance and when we arrived at the hospital were informed by a young and sympathetic doctor named Gibney, that Moya was dead.

Afterwards we had to break the news to my other two children – John and my younger daughter Erris. We spent a sleepless night. The first person we phoned the following morning was Frank Conroy in Killiney. He was stunned to silence. He was a great friend of Moya's and she of his. He said: 'I'll be down at half past eight.' He was.

My younger daughter Erris had told me that Moya once told her that life with me was not always smooth. It had its share of turbulence, but that nevertheless it was a great adventure. It pleased me to hear that.

To give an example of Moya's good humour and tolerance – and living with me required super-human tolerance – I recall one night on which there was a meeting of the Mayoman's Association in the old Jury's Hotel in Dame Street, during which there was a 'Question and Answer' session with a panel. The panel consisted of Miriam Hedermann-O'Brien; Sean Flanagan the Mayo footballer and former Connaught/Ulster MEP, Tony O'Reilly who was then in the milk sector and myself.

One of the questions put to us was what we thought of the nude painting in the Hugh Lane Gallery in Parnell Square. It was then something of a controversial topic in Dublin. Miriam Hedermann-O'Brien delivered quite a lengthy answer on art and its various forms; O'Reilly, who as well as being a great businessman is a wonderful raconteur, delivered a very witty answer; Sean Flanagan treated it all as if he was directing a football towards the appropriate goalposts. My reply, with Moya seated in the audience in front of me was 'pithy' and one to which grave exception could have been taken by a less equable woman. 'There is no doubt', I said 'that while the female form is a thing of beauty, yet nobody can regard it as a joy forever.' I was pleased to see her laugh as heartily as anybody else.

I was away from home a lot throughout our marriage travelling as a practising barrister on the Western Circuit and, even after taking silk, appearing at many criminal trials around the country. Furthermore I represented the people of North Mayo in Leinster House for fifteen years, happily at a distance of nearly 200 miles where this foul imposition of 'clinics' was never thrust upon me. But nonetheless, I visited different parts of my constituency about three weekends in every four. A constituency with lots of inlets is difficult to get around fully.

As I said, politics and law practice kept me travelling a lot of the time, so that the rearing, schooling and general care of our three children was left to Moya. They were all successful, John and Alison are lawyers and Erris is a teacher, and they are all now living happily with their spouses and their own children. The thing I regret most is that Moya never saw or enjoyed the company of our grandchildren.

When she died we learned something about what true friendships are. I put Frank Conroy top of the list. He was immeasurably kind. Although they are not related my friendship with another Conroy family brings me to Bronwyn; she effectively took on the minding of Erris who was nineteen when her mother died. Rita Maher was a tower of strength also.

Moya's death brought home to me my good fortune in having so many friends who were willing to help. For myself I bottled up my emotion and it was only when I read John Healy's tribute to Moya in the *Western Journal* that, sitting alone, the flood-gates burst, and I wept uncontrollably. I reproduce here John Healy's article. Even today it moves me, as almost nothing else can:

– Moya Lindsay was buried on Budget Day and the very elements, it seemed, grieved at the tragically sudden passing, as gale force winds buffeted the mourners of State and judiciary, as well as a big host of private friends from Mayo and Cavan and the counties adjoining.

For close on thirty years now Pat Lindsay has been a big man in Dublin; he has had his ups and downs in politics and through it all he remained the invulnerable Lindsay, once the Great Congest, now the successful barrister, again the great raconteur with the easy wit, gifted with a family as promising as any parent could wish and still the same Pat Lindsay who ran barefooted in Geesala, a safety-pin keeping the gansey closed against the winter wind, the country lad who had purchased the right to smoke a Havana cigar in Eamon Casey's pub without anyone thinking any less of him for it.

(L-R): V. Rev. James O'Reilly; Adm. Cavan, Self, Rev. Mgr. Thomas Faby who officiated, Moya and Rev. Paddy Reilly, Columbian Fathers, her cousin (1952)

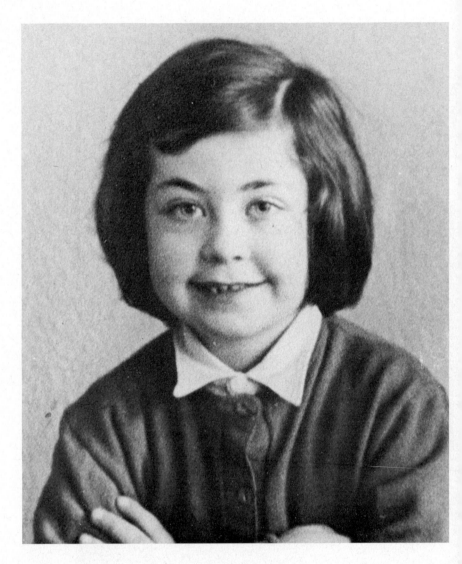

My youngest daughter Erris

With daughter Alison after her call to the Bar
30.07.1975

Retirement, 18.01.1984

(L-R): Son John, Anthony Collins, V.President of Incorporated Law Society; Self; Paddy McEntee S.C., President of Bar Council and Peter Sutherland S.C., Attorney General

*Picture used in General Election 1954 when I was
first elected for the then North Mayo constituency*

Judge Charles S. Wyse Power

Retired as Master of the High Court, 18.01.1984

(L-R): Patrick McEntee S.C., President of the Bar Council, Self and Peter Sutherland, Attorney-General later to become our commissioner in the E.C.

Paying Attention

With the Irish delegation to the Inter Parliamentary Union Vienna 1954

Interparliamentary Union, Helsinki, 1955

(L-R): The late Sean Lemass, The late P.J. Little a former Fianna Fáil Minister; Self; and Sir Malcolm Stoddart Scott, Tory M.P and Leader of the British Delegation

(L-R): Self, John A. Costello, Sean T. O'Kelly and General R. Mulcahy, 1956

With Chiang Kai Shek in Taipei ,1960
He presented me with his book 'Communist Russia in China'

With the late President Johnson of Liberia in Tokyo, 1960

With Liam Cosgrave, 1966

*Exchanging anecdotes of a Cork by-election in 1956
at the opening of the extension of Law Library*

My portrait in U.C.G.

Self and cousin Eamon Lindsay, Federal MP for Herbert Federal Parliament of Australia

Lindsay, with practical Moya at his side, telling him not to be daft when she thought it was right, laughing at him now and again and saying, with a smile in her eye: "Will ye look at him?" seemed invulnerable.

'I know few women who so complemented a man as did Moya complement Pat Lindsay for if Pat ever tended to overdo the urbane bit Moya would puncture the performance with a nod of the head: "Will ye listen to him" and Pat, smiling with the rest could only say "Yes".

She helped him through a bad patch or two in politics and just as important, his friends would go to her to be helped over a bad patch of their own. Anyone who was in a doghouse could go to Moya Lindsay and the practical wife and mother in her – the essential goodness you get in a fine woman – sorted their problems out for them with basic commonsense. As we say at home, Moya had no side to her and was loved all the more for it. A decade ago she had her own trouble and she made light of it and it passed: it was a time of rejoicing. She had the pleasure of seeing her daughter Alison, follow in Pat's footsteps as a barrister and later of marrying, of seeing John and Erris follow sure-footed in Alison's first footsteps to maturity.

She saw Pat's elevation to the bench and delighted as much in his friend's celebration of the achievement as she did in Pat's accomplishment. With the family just about reared they enjoyed a pleasant social life together; they had a cottage in Connemara which was a nice hide-away for both of them and the last time we talked – at the launch of Ted Nealon's *Guide to the 21st Dail and Senate* book which is now a best seller – she was full of the renovation plans she had. She got this winter a set out for making curtains and drapes for the cottage and by the summer everything would be finished. They were together, as always, in Galway on the last weekend and were returning home and had reached the outskirts of Dublin. She died in Pat's arms and those of her daughter Alison and it was hard – very hard – to see how vulnerable the old Great Congest was.

The face was brave, as men like James Dillon, Liam Cosgrave, his cabinet ministers, members of the Bar Library, the judiciary, newspaper friends, political associates and family friends sympathised; the half-smoked Havana, the vital nod of the head and even the smile, were all there. Pat was taking it well. But the eyes alone failed to hide the grievous, sudden, awful, sense of loss...'

* * * *

I was never someone who was careful about money. As my father once said to me: 'One might as well say that money is round and your great propensity is to make it go round' but Moya was quite different. She had a business training and had been brought up by parents who were in business. One evening during the course of a financial conversation – a conversation I never welcomed – Moya remarked: 'I don't think you are able to handle money.' 'Perhaps you're right,' I said, 'do you have any suggestions?' 'I think I should take over the accounts' she answered. 'Alright' I said, rationalising that I did not have to give her every cheque I got. However it soon transpired that I was getting less pocket money than my son. But one day I got a very sizeable cheque which I did not hand over. I cashed it and proceeded to enjoy myself with my friends.

Eventually I went home. I had a habit of always going in to my two daughters to kiss them goodnight whether they were asleep or awake, and whether I was sober or not. This particular night feeling expansive, I gave them each a tenner. At that time my pocket money aside from petrol and an allowance for cigars was only a tenner.

Characteristically, little Erris put her tenner under her pillow, while Alison secreted hers in her handbag. The following day Moya found the £10 note under Erris's pillow. Later that day when she asked her where she had got it, Erris told her.

The following Saturday morning when my pocket money was being distributed Moya said to me: 'Well you deserve yours because I don't believe there is anybody else could save £20 out of £10.' The game was up.

The trouble for me really started when I became Master of the High Court and I was only getting one cheque per fortnight. Fortunately, the occasional cheque kept coming in which saved me from penury.

About three weeks after Moya's death Erris asked; 'Daddy, who is going to pay the bills now – the bills Mummy used to pay?'

'I suppose I will.'

'Well now, if Mummy couldn't trust you with the cheque book I don't know if I can' she retorted.

I reminded her that she was only nineteen and I did not know what attitude the Bank Manager might have to her proposal. But I told her I had no objection in her going to see him.

The arrangements were made for a visit to the bank, an occasion I always look back on with amusement. There I was, sitting in the corner of the bank manager's office, while he and Erris were deciding business and the signing of bankers orders. I felt like a priviledged chauffeur who had been allowed into the room.

Erris handled our finances just as well as her mother, but with one improvement not to my advantage; I had to hand her the stubs of my lodgements. By this time she was earning her own salary as a primary school teacher. 'Daddy, don't you get another stub with your official cheque which shows deductions, various payments, tax-free allowances and that sort of thing?'

'I do of course.'

'Well, I'd like to see it.'

I produced the most recent one. 'That's alright', she said.

'What's alright?'

'I just wanted to see if you were lodging the net amounts on that counterfoil you are showing me.'

Part II

The Law

I have written elsewhere that I began my career at University College Galway without the benefit of any career guidance, so I naturally took on the subjects I liked best. Consequently when I finished up in 1937 with my Masters Degree in Ancient Classics, I had the education of a gentleman, but one for which there was little market and, as I was to discover the hard way, I was not really cut out to be a teacher.

I was not long in Galway before I discovered the Courthouse. I was in lodgings in Wood Quay and every day I passed the Courthouse on my way to the university. Indeed, leaving the lodgings on the first day I attended university, and asking the way, we were told that the University was the first big building across the bridge. We knocked at the door of this rather gaunt building and the fellow inside shot a little slide open and we enquired if this was the University. He said: 'No, this is the County Jail – you're not ready for this place yet.' The jail is the site on which the present Cathedral stands.

But we were passing the Courthouse everyday and attracted by crowds on certain days I, as it were, followed the crowd and eventually got into the public gallery and immediately became fascinated by this scene. The judge was sitting up on a high bench wearing a wig, black gown and a crimson sash which denoted that he was holding Criminal trials – something I only discovered afterwards.

This judge was a great man called Charles Wyse Power. His mother Jennie Wyse Power was later a member of the Senate. He was a good looking man, with a great appearance, good voice and very quick to get to the point. He disposed of trials with great rapidity. He was one of two judges who continued to wear the crimson sash. The other was Judge Gleeson on the Midland Circuit which included the Longford,

Roscommon and Sligo area. They continued to wear the sash as a relic I suppose, or going as far as they could go with the formal British tradition of colour. I always thought the Irish Bar and the Judiciary were extremely foolish to drop the trappings of justice's wearing these criminal sashes in Criminal Trials. Just look at the many successful organisations of the world, particularly the Great Communion of Rome where they have dropped nothing except the black vestments in two thousand years. They are still going strong in spite of it and in spite of some of their members.

However it was the sense of theatre about the courts which appealed to me. I was, as I have mentioned, at this stage very involved in the Dramatic Societies in Galway and the court to me was simply an extension of this – almost a real life enactment. I was fascinated, not just by Judge Wyse Power, but also by some of the barristers, men like Denis Johnston (later a famous playwright and wartime broadcaster) and Kevin Haugh, addressing juries or addressing the judge from time to time. After three or four Circuit Criminal Courts I became quite *au fait* with the whole procedure and determined that if I ever got a chance that would be the career in which I would finish up. In fact it would not be exaggerating to say that by the time I finished at Galway my overriding ambition was to go into the Law, but I knew that it was not going to be easy and that there was a long arduous road ahead of me, with no tradition in my family of law, something which was regarded as very important at that time.

My interest in the Law continued, especially in my reading books concerning the great murder trials and other celebrated legal matters. As a spectator in the Galway Circuit Court I didn't then regard solicitors as very important but, of course, in that I was quite wrong, because they were the people who were feeding Counsel with briefs containing the necessary information to present their cases. For me, however, it was the Bar or nothing.

One of my reasons for leaving Cavan and going to Dublin was to try to realise this ambition. I knew that even if I had the money when I was in Galway, the Galway Law School wasn't then recognised as a first year course. At that time I could do the Law course in three years – one year at university, either UCD or Trinity whichever I chose, and the remaining two years in King's Inns. That I felt would be easy as far as a job was concerned, because the lectures in the King's Inns were from 4.30 - 5.30 p.m. and 5.30 - 6.30 p.m. four days a week.

And so, while teaching at Sandford Park I started my first year at UCD in 1943. My professors were Daniel Binchy, Patrick McGilligan and Michael Ryan. Excellent as they were I never took that year seriously, largely because it interfered with my earning process. But notes were generously available from other students and attendance wasn't a very strict requirement. In fact it was quite common that people would answer the roll for others and in the large class it was never really noticed.

I then moved on to spend two years in King's Inns where, with a fair degree of mediocrity around, I had two wonderful people as lecturers. One was Ignatius Kelly, whose father was a native of Castlebar and had been Solicitor General for Ireland. Ignatius was a barrister who never took silk, had an extraordinary grasp of case law, in both contract and tort, but would digress at the drop of a hat to talk about the Connaught Rangers.

The other lecturer was Professor Frances Moran. She was part of the family which owned Moran's Hotel in Talbot Street. She was one of the first women to go to Trinity, not as a class-conscious Catholic but as a woman asserting her rights. She had a lecturing practice with which I disagreed, though largely I suppose because for students it was profoundly disconcerting. In every third lecture she would, for the first twenty minutes ask random questions on the subjects of the two previous lectures. For some odd reason I made up my mind that I wasn't going to answer these, but I knew perfectly well that refusing them would get me into trouble so I sought the easier way by simply replying to every question: 'I don't know.'

One day, however, around the eighth or ninth lecture in the first year, she came in rather briskly for her 4.30 p.m. lecture, and called the roll, which began, with my great friend, now deceased, Circuit Court Judge Stephen Barrett. After Barrett came Blaney, the Blaney in question being Alice Blaney, the wife of the present Chief Justice Tom Finlay. And so on, having finished her roll call Professor Moran looked at us rather quizzically and said: 'I often thought that Justinian would not have been the man he was if it were not for his wonderful wife, Theodora. Does anybody here know anything about Theodora?' Mine was the only hand to shoot up. Naturally, from my study of the Ancient Classics, I knew all about Theodora. Professor Moran said: 'Lindsay knows something,' adding, 'tell us about Theodora.' So I told the story of Theodora, completely unexpurgated. She looked at me, again rather quizzically and said: 'Accurately if indelicately told.'

We became friends from that date. Whenever I think of the word Theodora it doesn't bring to mind cookery lessons or anything like that; it reminds me of Professor Frances Moran. She remained my friend until her death many years afterwards and was of considerable help to me in the Law Library when I ultimately went in.

I wasn't a great student, in part because at that time I made up my mind (I think rightly, without any logical process involved in this thinking) that the examinations didn't really matter as far as ultimate practice and procedure was concerned. In fact, we didn't do practice and procedure in King's Inns or anywhere else in those days, so when I came into the Law Library I didn't know what a Writ was, or a Civil Bill. I knew nothing about pleadings. The men who really guided me along in these matters were firstly, Charlie Conroy, later to become a Circuit Judge and then John A. Costello who was then the busiest man in the Library, but never too busy to offer a helping hand to even the most junior member.

Much has been said and written about the famous King's Inns dinners but this was during the War and dinners had been suspended. As a result I was deprived of the opportunity of learning to eat and hold my drink like a gentleman. Consequently I had never had dinners until long after I was called to the Bar, and then very rarely, because we hadn't been brought through the process of having dinners during my student days.

Life was difficult, but after my years of poverty, near-hunger, part-time teaching, odd jobs here and there and eventually the security of Sandford Park, I knew exactly what I wanted and I was determined that I was going to stick it out at the Bar. I had now scraped a few pounds together and was helped by the substantial help which Professor Michael Tierney, later President of UCD and then Professor of Greek at that University was able to give me as I have already recounted. He was however to do me a further kindness at this time. He appointed me as the tutor and guardian to Eoin MacWhite whose father was then the Irish Ambassador to the Vatican and was, because of wartime circumstances, virtually a prisoner there. I was appointed to look after Eoin and to tutor him in Greek. The proceeds from this paid the rent on my flat and even left a few pounds over each week. Eoin and I became great friends. He was an extraordinarily gifted Classicist and later became our ambassador to Australia.

* * * *

I was called to the Bar on what I always think is a significant date – the Feast of All Saints, the first of November 1946.

I had to get a gown and some winged collars and bands. My wig, I bought for the equivalent of £1.50 today – and it was an old horse hair wig, a genuine article, very dirty, very stained, it belonged to the late Mr Justice Dodd when he was a Sergeant at Law. I believe he had practiced around the Limerick area. The wig was of vital importance but it was also important to get it as cheaply as possible. This particular wig lasted for nearly forty years. It didn't look great, but it looked experienced.

* * * *

In 1946 I made my first appearance as a barrister in the Circuit Court in Belmullet, which I regard as my hometown, although I lived ten miles south of it. Incidently there was no welcoming of anybody to the Bar in those days; you just came, appeared and the County Registrar probably told the judge who you were, if he didn't know already.

I had one application. It was an old Section 52 application under the Land Registry Law, now gone, the same as Workman's Compensation. It was things like this which helped juniors along in those days even if at a guinea or two a time. They are all gone now.

I got through that application successfully. It was only a question of reading an affidavit but, in spite of all the experience I had of acting and public speaking, I found it unnerving. It was all the more so in that I had been practicing my voice projection for some time and developing my interest in voice, right up to the court. I had a high regard for the importance of the voice. I had read somewhere, when I was thirteen of fourteen, about Demosthenes practicing against the roar of the waves with a pebble in his mouth. I tried that on the shore at home, and I damn near succeeded in choking myself.

In any event I got through the Belmullet Circuit Court application, the only thing I had to do that day. The fee was two guineas, paid promptly by the Solicitor on the day. As I was coming out of the tiny Bar room in the Courthouse on the way to lunch, I bumped into the judge quite accidently. I immediately apologised to the judge who was the same Charles Wyse Power, the man I had been fascinated by in Galway thirteen or fourteen years before: 'You're Lindsay, the new man?'

'Yes, My Lord.'

'Walk up the street with me to the hotel. It will do you no harm to be seen walking with the judge in your home town.'

I thought that was a very generous gesture. I walked up the street with him and he was right. It did me no harm, because the whole town was talking about it for days, maybe weeks afterwards.

Belmullet was the last round up of that winter circuit, so I came back to Dublin and I went into the Law Library. The fee per annum was then eight guineas – two for the Robing Room and six for the use of the Library. An interesting thing about the Law Library was the efficiency, helpfulness and courtesy of what they called the attendents, the book boys. Their knowledge was quite extraordinary. If you asked them for a book dealing with any particular kind of problem, they would immediately find the correct text book.

When I went in there was an extraordinary man on the rostrum inside the door. Nobody can pass through the doors of the Law Library except barristers, book boys and cleaners. Not even a solicitor can pass the rostrum. He must name the barrister he's looking for and is called by the person in charge. Anyhow, there was this extraordinary man – extraordinary by reason of his voice. He would put the personality of the person called into the way he pronounced his name. His name was Campion; there's a story that a senior named Robert Hogan one day went up to Campion and said: 'Campion, I'm in a dreadful hurry and I have a junior, I forget his name, but it's like an address in Terenure.' Whereupon Campion turned around to the general library and loudly intoned: 'Weldon Parke.'

There were two other fine book boys in the Law Library – Tommy Whelan and Pat Redmond. For the 29 years that I was in the Library, Tommy Whelan was my guide and mentor. He kept me out of trouble. I often drove him home and we had a few pints in the '51', Tom Ryan's public house on Haddington Road.

During my whole life I was never class conscious or snobbish – how could I be! – even when I reached a group that would regard themselves as a superior class. I think everybody is important, and particularly the boys at the library, the doormen, hotel porters, the guard on the beat, the cinema usher and usherettes, barmen. Generally they are better to know than the chairman of the board of directors.

Of course things change and have changed. I went back to the Law Library in the 1980s after leaving the Mastership of the High Court with the intention of rejoining. I was still active and clear in my mind and I still loved the challenge, which I missed heavily during my period as Master. So I went in, turned left at the rostrum, over to what was called the smoking bay where I used to sit, and found all the bookshelves covered with heavy mesh and secured with padlocks.

This was not the Law Library that I left and I didn't rejoin. Somebody was stealing the books – barristers perhaps. Certainly I don't think that the other groups that could get in there, the cleaning women and the book boys would steal them. They would hardly do it because they wouldn't have a sale for them. Barristers would certainly have a use for them.

Between then and Christmas not very much really happened. I had no work, but I was finding my way around the Library, getting to know people. The library is very much like a secondary school. In your first year you know everybody. It's only as you advance up the years that you forget the juniors coming in. You don't know them as well.

I have no experience of British Chambers but I rather imagine it would be better if Chambers were available here. In fact, I often expressed the view that when the Henrietta Street buildings were for sale the Benchers should have tried to purchase them and convert them into Chambers. It would have been quite convenient to Green Street and the Four Courts.

* * * *

The Law Library was a great place in those days. It was full of people with specialised knowledge who never refused to part with that knowledge to a junior in search of help. Let me illustrate that point. I remember one day getting a brief from P. Hogan and Company of Ballinasloe (the original office of Patrick Hogan, the former Minister for Agriculture). Patrick Hogan had been practicing with Vincent Shields of Loughrea but they split up the partnership; Hogan took Ballinasloe and Mountbellew, Shields took Loughrea and Athenry.

In any event I got this extraordinary case, read it, and was no wiser at the end. The query to me was something concerning the rights of tenants for life, vis-a-vis growing trees. Well now, you might as well have presented me with the biggest jigsaw in the world and I would probably have had more success with the jigsaw. So I started to wander around, as was the custom in the library at the time, asking different people who might know something about growing trees and tenants for life, all of which was very vague to me. Eventually I was directed towards a charming, rotund, pink-faced little Protestant from the North of Ireland called Charlie Campbell. Charlie said: 'Have you got an hour to spare?'

I said I had several hours to spare. He said 'Bring over your notebook.' So I complied, brought over the notebook and started to write at his dictation various points in connection with 'tenants for life'. It became a little clearer to me as he was going along, and he said: 'Now go back and write your opinion.'

So I went back and based on those notes I wrote an opinion which I re-read and also considered advice I had got a few weeks earlier from Thomas J. Connolly, one of the most brilliant men that I knew at the Irish Bar, if not *the* most brilliant. (He was a brother of the late Ann McGilligan and died just a short time ago). He told me that when you get some case to advise, you should ask yourself what the law ought to be, if you didn't know what it was, and you will find that your commonsense, in 99.9 per cent of cases, will tell you what the law actually is.

Now, remembering that advice, and reading the opinion I had written, I said to myself, this doesn't sound right. There's something wrong here. So I enquired from a few people, including the late Desmond Bell who told me: 'There's an Irish case on that. I don't know what year it is, but you will get it in the index or in the digests. It's *Gilmore and the O'Connor Don.*'

So I said to myself at this point, why I hadn't thought of this before, especially since I knew the plaintiff, Jack Gilmore. I didn't know anything about the O'Connor Don, except that he was one of the last High Kings of Ireland. So I read the case, particularly the judgement of the Irish Supreme Court – which was the exact opposite of what Charlie Campbell had told me. And, to my further surprise, looking at the appearances at the bottom, Charlie Campbell was the leader in the losing side.

I thought that maybe this had slipped his memory and I thought in fairness to him and in view of the time he had given me that I should go back to him and remind him of this. I did so. And he looked at me and laughed and said: 'The Supreme Court was quite wrong.'

That was the day that I said: 'Would to God for ten minutes in the House of Lords.'

* * * *

The first case of any significance in which I was a junior (with the late Kevin Kenny as my senior) was a famous 'Dog Trial' from Galway. Five men had been returned for trial to the next sitting of the Galway Circuit Criminal Court. In those days, prosecuting counsel could apply without notice for a transfer to the Central Criminal Court in Dublin. This was promptly done, and one could well understand the reason – it would be difficult to get a conviction from a Galway jury in relation to greyhounds.

Now the indictment against my client, and the other four, was the same, namely that they had conspired together to run a dog at the Galway racetrack on the 'X' day of 1946, which purported to be 'Funny Fish' but was not in fact 'Funny Fish'. That was the indictment as drafted by the late Mr John Willie O'Connor, the prosecution claiming that there was in fact substitution.

John Willie O' Connor handed the indictment in turn to the senior counsel, the late Sean Hooper who added to the indictment, 'but was Red Jack'. Seniors like doing things like that, putting in a comma, adding a word here or there, or changing 'and' to 'or' – just to show their little bit of superiority. In this case, this particular addition, 'but was Red Jack' was fatal to the prosecution case.

We were transferred to Dublin and, after some days hearing three of the accused were acquitted by direction, on the evidence that had been given. The case of the remaining two, one of them my client, went to the jury and the jury convicted. I'll never forget it. It was a Friday and we expected to get off.

In spite of our pleas the late Judge Davitt said they would have to go to Mountjoy for the weekend. He would give them bail on Monday because he was going to give a certificate of Leave to Appeal, as he thought the point being made on submissions to him was of public importance. The point was that it was necessary to prove the whole of an indictment, not a part. The State had proved beyond any shadow of a doubt that the dog purporting to be 'Funny Fish' was not 'Funny Fish' but they failed to prove it was 'Red Jack'.

That point was thought of first by Declan Quigley who was then practicing on the Circuit and in this case he was a junior with Chris Micks – and Chris Micks very generously attributed the point of a submission to Declan Quigley who later became permanent head of the Attorney General's office, and is now in retirement.

So our clients spent the weekend in Mountjoy, which didn't please them very much, but we came up before the court of Criminal Appeal on the Monday who upheld the verdict of the jury, but they, in turn, granted us a certificate of Leave to Appeal to the Supreme Court and we went to the Supreme Court and there it was found that the conviction was defective because it was not the result of the proof of the whole of the indictment. So we got off.

I'll never forget our seniors asking for costs ... We were nearly all sent to Mountjoy.

I had never put a bet on a dog in my life. But, as a student, I used to frequent the old Royal Hotel in Eyre Square in Galway and I did take part in 'doggy jobs' in the yard of the hotel – simply holding a dog while sombody would paint a white bit on his tail, or give him a star on the breast, or put a rubber band on his toes to affect his speed. So when I got into that trial, I wasn't under any illusion about things that happened at the Galway racetrack and probably at several others.

* * * *

In 1948 I had my first prosecution in Galway. It was a very long trial and it was my first experience of that wonderful character who was then State Solicitor in Galway, Jasper Kelly. Just before I rose to open the case to the jury my gown was plucked. It was Jasper Kelly – my instructing solicitor – saying to me that he was going out for about twenty minutes. That was a Wednesday morning. The next time I saw my State solicitor was when the jury retired on the following Friday. That was Jasper's first great disappearance in my life.

He was, however, a generous man and it didn't come as a great surprise to me in 1950 – although it was a shock – when, while on holidays at my parents home in Mayo, totally devoid of text books of any kind, I got a brief from Jasper which bore the magic title: 'Murder'.

My job was to go to Galway on a certain day and take depositions in the District Court from the Garda file.

Now I had no idea as to how I should set about taking depositions. But I went to Galway and I was in the courthouse at 10 a.m. The court wasn't sitting for the purpose of taking depositions until 12 o'clock, and I knew that there was, in some office in Galway, a very fine copy of a Criminal Law text book called *Criminal Law Practice and Procedure* written by a man called Robert Linsley Sandys. I also knew that there was a chapter in that book devoted entirely to the making of depositions.

Standing alone in the Bar room of the Galway courthouse I felt very uncomfortable, because I didn't have a copy of Sandys. But I did hear a very familiar heavy footstep, and my heart jumped. Here was aid. It was Jasper Kelly, the State solicitor, my instructing solicitor who was instructing me in this particular matter: 'Jasper I'm delighted to see you.'

'Ha, Ha' says he.

'Would you have a copy of Sandys' *Criminal Law*?'

'Ha, Ha' says Jasper. 'The sands of the desert grow cold.'

Whereupon he turned on his heel and walked away. I never saw him during the course of that case again.

But with the help of the Guards and, indeed the solicitor on the other side, Bill Gavin, we managed to do a very good job over two days. The presiding judge, the late Walter Moloney, was helpful and kind.

The case concerned a murder by a man of his wife, on an island in Connemara, not far from where I live now. I will always remember a Guard Doherty who came out to the island and single-handedly took statements, kept the accused under control and did a mighty job of police work.

The trial was conducted entirely in Irish, and it was my first time hearing the word 'craiceann' being used for sex. I always thought the word was 'gneas'. In fact I have since discovered another word, 'collaíocht'. Eventually when the case came to the Central Criminal Court the accused was found unfit to plead.

Twenty years later, I'm standing in line for the Sunday papers at Michael Tom Folan's shop in the same district and a man immediately in front of me announced his order.

'Tabhairim twenty Major agus páipéar craiceann'

I wondered what would happen but he got his twenty Major and the *News Of The World* so, even in Irish speaking districts, they know what kind of English should be read.

* * * *

Over the years numerous people have asked me if it was difficult taking on a case where you know or suspected that your client was guilty as charged, but you still had to defend him. I always made the same reply: 'It is not a difficulty. The ethics of the matter are simple, according to the advice given to me by the late James Fitzgerald Kenny.' He said: 'Never refuse a prisoner's brief. You defend that prisoner in spite of what suspicions you might have as to his guilt or otherwise, right up to the end of the State case, simply to try and break down the State case. Now if you get acquitted at that stage, fair enough. If you're not, the ethics require you not to put the accused into the box to give false evidence,' and I have been extremely successful in several cases, mainly murder trials, in not putting the accused into the box, irrespective of what I thought.

Over my career I was involved in 39 murder trials, prosecuting in 4 and defending in 35. Of that 35 I was convicted twice, 8 verdicts of manslaughter were brought in and the remainder were found not guilty, which I believe is a pretty good record. Perhaps it also raises the question of the abolition of the death penalty. I have never been an abolitionist. I do believe that the death penalty is a deterrent.

I recall one case in which I defended a fellow who was accused of murdering a child by drowning. The evidence coming from the State's side was that the accused came out of a public house, was drunk and fell on the footpath and it depended on which way he was facing when he got up, as to what direction he would take. As it was, he went off and met a neighbour's child and bought sweets for him and they went for a walk on the bank of a river and nobody ever really knew what happened, but the child was drowned.

Now I maintained by way of submission to the judge, that this was a classic case following the principal of *R. versus Reed* way back in the early 1900s whereby, if a man was found to be so incapacitated by drink as not to be able to form the intent of committing a crime, that he shouldn't be convicted of it.

The late George Murnaghan who was presiding in this case would have none of that. He had been a famous prosecutor in his time, and he remained so on the bench. My client was convicted and Judge Murnaghan sentenced him to death by hanging. I didn't feel that there was any great advantage in appealing. The facts of the case were clear enough. But I did think that this was a case where the death sentence should be commuted to one of penal servitude for life.

This happened shortly after I had left Government and I was very friendly with one of the most decent men in this country, Maurice Moynihan, then Secretary to the Government. I rang him up and asked him was there a possibility of getting it onto the Government Agenda within the next few days. At that time we had only four days in which to appeal in writing, the appeal being signed by the prisoner. So two days later he rang me at the Law Library and told me that the sentence had been commuted to penal servitude for life.

I immediately sat into my car and drove up to Mountjoy jail to meet the fine big bulk of a man that I had last seen three days previously. Now his clothes were flapping around him – he had lost about three stone in weight during that short space of time. So when people tell me that the death penalty is not a deterrent, I always think of him.

* * * *

Earlier, when the Criminal Justice Bill abolishing capital punishment was brought in front of the Houses of the Oireacthas, I was in the Senate. As everybody knows the death penalty was retained for the killing of a police officer on duty, a prison warden or an ambassador. I considered this daft because if you killed a policeman in the course of a riot or fracas or during the commission of a crime it was capital murder deserving the death penalty, whereas if some public-spirited citizen went to the assistance of the police, it was non-capital murder. I thought that the logic was very defective. Anyhow, I had in my own mind, as a result of my experience and knowledge of different happenings, that there should be other cases included that would deserve the death penalty. I was particularly concerned that the death penalty be retained for anybody convicted of murder by poisoning or pre-meditated killing.

Within one month of that Senate debate, with my position on poisoners well known, I was briefed to appear for an alleged poisoner where the vehicle through which the poison had allegedly been conveyed was a pot of tea. After a conviction in the first trial, I successfully got a new trial in the Court of Criminal Appeal by reason of the fact that the judge had misdirected himself in law. In two subsequent trials the juries failed to agree and thus the accused was acquitted.

Some time later I was asked as to my private view on the guilt, or not, of the accused. I replied: '"Not Guilty" on the verdict of twelve good men and true.' I then added: 'If, however, I were offered a cup of tea in that house, I would be very slow to take it.'

* * * *

The murder cases were always the most fascinating, because the challenge was formidable. A man's or a woman's life was at stake during the death penalty period or else it was a matter of a long prison sentence, so one had to do one's best to see that justice was done. In every courthouse, in the course of every case, whether counsel is acting for a plaintiff or a defendant, there is only one important person in the whole courtroom, and that is one's client. One must take every step within the law, and within of course, a moral code, to see that he or she gets full justice.

I have often been blamed for grovelling to judges and to the jury – I did. This was quite deliberate, because I believed it was in the best interest of my client.

My attitude to the conduct of a case was greatly influenced by advice I got very early on in my career from Charles Wyse Power. He said: 'In every case, no matter how complicated, there is one net point. Find it.' Secondly, I was influenced by advice from Joseph A. McCarthy, a Circuit Court judge in Dublin, who was one of the best criminal lawyers that I ever came across – and father of the late, and justly lamented, Supreme Court judge Niall McCarthy. He said: 'Look at every exhibit, every piece of evidence, you can never examine evidence too carefully or too often, look at it front, back and often.' And thirdly, I had discovered that judges and juries have their Achilles heels. I found in particular with the judiciary, that their Achilles heel was vanity. I have often played up to that very successfully on behalf of my clients.

* * * *

There was one rape case among the many which I defended which stands out in my memory. It took place in Galway very early in my career and the complainant, or the victim as she would now be called, was a girl of about twenty-five or twenty-six. I was defending the accused who stoutly, during consultation, protested his innocence. When I explained to him that, once she was over seventeen and consented, then it wasn't a crime, but that consent had to be fully given, in the full knowledge of what was happening.

So he said: 'Is that the law?'

I said, 'It is. Now, have you any different view?'

'Ah, sure the whole village was with her.'

'In that case, why not you also?'

'Well,' he said, 'if you say that's what the law is, I was.'

This case took place just after the second World War and at that time the whole question of rubber and elastic was very important, largely because it was in short supply, and, what there was, was defective. Even tyres for bicycles and motor cars were not up to standard and the same applied to elastic as used in clothing. During the woman's evidence she said her undergarments were removed by force. In the course of examination I asked her: 'Were they new?' She said: 'Yes,' which meant that the elastic was bound to be defective. Then I went into a series of questions with her about pre-war and post-war elastic in relation to ladies underwear, and I wanted to know, as a final question: 'Why, if all the struggle you say took place, why was it that this obviously defective elastic wasn't broken?' And she gave me a surprising answer. She said: 'I lifted it myself' which established consent and my client was acquitted.

When the trial was over, the judge's crier, a man called Cox, came to me and said the judge would like to see me. It was again Charles Wyse Power. He said: 'Lindsay where did you find out about the strengths of pre-war and post-war elastic?'

'I have four sisters, My Lord'

'Sorry for asking' he said, and that was that.

Rape trials were not reported then and I think that the current reporting of them contains one dangerous element – if you report the name of the convicted person it might well lead to the identity of the victim. That certainly would not be a good thing for her, because, she would, in accordance with the puritanical manner that still exists, be regarded as being somewhat at fault, and her reputation might suffer accordingly.

* * * *

The best jury in my experience was a Dublin jury. I am talking of course about the juries of the days gone by, not since the Supreme Court went mad and gave everybody on the Voters' List the right to be a juror. That was the second time they went daft – the first time was when they gave bail in the O'Callaghan case and gave us our present crazy situation where crimes are committed almost with impunity, by people on bail. Indeed it is well known that there have been people who have robbed banks on their way home from court, having just got bail.

I never had a woman on a jury, they had not come in at that stage, and I regret that. However, you couldn't ask for better than twelve good men and true, particularly in the country. If you had a man with a tunic shirt, with the neck open and a blue-stained collar with stud showing, he was sound. He was the man to address during all proceedings. There was a certain reasonableness about him and he was, in my experience, the one man on the jury who took the greatest interest. I have seen jurors looking bored and when they look bored you're in trouble. You've got to rouse them. So the fellow with the blue-collar stud was the man. If you had him on your side, your chance of success was high.

* * * *

I remember once defending a man in Green Street Courthouse who was on legal aid. Through all my career I was never one for long speeches. What I had to say I could certainly say in a maximum of twenty minutes. Sometimes if you had to review evidence, you might have to go on longer, say in a difficult technical case. But on this particular day I had been succinct – and successful.

Two wags (professional court watchers), leaving the public gallery in Green Street and one said to the other: 'There's legal aid for you. I often heard Lindsay talking for an hour – eleven and a half minutes today.'

* * * *

One of the greatest cases I remember was a murder trial from Mayo, my junior was the late Ben O'Quigley and our instructing solicitor was the late Paddy McEllin from Claremorris.

It was a simple enough story where a young local country lad, who had been to school for only forty-six days in his life, was charged. According to the evidence he had reached the pinnacle of fame, because he was 'doing a line' as they say, or 'keeping company' with a clerk in the local post-office. However, a 'Mission' had come to the village and with it had come the Mission stall, with its holy pictures, relics, rosaries, scapulars and the like. Within a few days the young lady had started going out with the man who ran the Mission stall. My client, on discovering this, lost his head, and in the ensuing row, the young lady was killed. The evidence was overwhelming and the best we could hope for was a manslaughter verdict. As I concluded my short address to the jury I said to them: 'Imagine my client's disappointment, his despair, when he didn't meet her in the accustomed place but found her instead in a darkened alleyway with an oily-haired peddler of religious objects at the local Mission stalls.'

Immediately after I had sat down, Paddy McEllin and Ben O'Quigley whispered to me: 'You went too far.' I said: 'Do you ever look at anything? There are five fellows in that jury wearing Trinity ties and they would never have a lot of time for scapulars or Missions.'

I got my manslaughter verdict.

* * * *

The one thing I want to say about judges, irrespective of the source of their appointment, is that I always found them, with one or two exceptions, in certain cases only, to be fair and equitable. I learned a lot from good judges. When I think of good judges I put Charles Wyse Power first. Closely behind him I put Joseph A. McCarthy whom I have mentioned already and the late Judge Henry Shannon. Not alone were they good judges but they looked like judges. They had substance and they were very gentlemanly. The late Cearbhall O'Dalaigh was the embodiment of politeness and was very kind to juniors. So was Conor Maguire, the previous Chief Justice. John Kenny was both a polite and courteous judge, as well as a good lawyer.

There were a lot of people who thought that the late Sean Butler was a disaster, but in my view, his was the nearest approach to Charles Wyse Power that I ever came across. The only difference was that while he always recognised the net point, he wanted counsel to find it faster. He was a great man to assimilate facts and he had a great knowledge of the law. He died tragically young.

On the negative side, I was not impressed by Judge George Murnaghan. And I should have been, because he was a very bright man and had been one of the great criminal lawyers of my time. As the late John Durkan said about Chris Micks, not alone was he worth watching but he had to be watched. Much the same was true of George Murnaghan. But he was rude, gratuitously rude. Vanity was his trouble. He was one of the great vain judges of my time. I think he had been passed over so often for the Supreme Court that the effect made him worse almost by the day.

As I talk about lawyers and judges memories come flooding back, the memory of Charles Wyse Power, waiting for me one day in Ballina, outside the hotel. He was going up to his last day's hearing and he said: 'Lindsay, I've been waiting for you. I cannot walk up that bloody hill.' I got him into the car and drove him up to the court. He went in and heard his cases, and went off in the train that evening accompanied by his wife Hinnie, who was always with him. He died that night. I missed him very much.

Then, after his death we had on the Western Circuit a succession of temporary invasions from different judges. We had Barra O'Briain, who was highly technical, cold and looked thoroughly indifferent to what was going on. We also had a fellow called Judge Martin Connolly who was the martinet of judges. I considered giving back all my briefs (and I had a considerable amount of them at that time) when I heard that Martin Connolly was down because he was such a pernickety fellow. He was a native of Connemara, but he always referred to the Connemara people as 'they are a strong people' – distancing himself from them.

He was a fine build of a man who dressed well and I recall my first day before him. I had strong reservations about appearing, but I said that I would give it a try.

That day the first person up was Seamus Henchy. He was crucified by Connolly.

Next was John Willie O'Connor. He too was crucified.

Then came Conor Maguire – later to work with the European Commission and now a disc jockey with a programme called *In The Mood* on R.T.E. (I'm told it's quite a good programme). He too got a battering.

I was fourth and I'll always remember it. It was a motion of a title. Connolly looked at me over the glasses and said: 'Are your proofs in order?'

'Yes My Lord, subject to your searching scrutiny.'

He looked at me with a wan smile, and said: 'I'm very glad you know that.'

I didn't go wrong for the next fortnight.

* * * *

When I came to Galway in 1947 for the January sittings, my first brief came from the old friend of my student days in politics, Michael J. Allen, of McDermot and Allen. The office is still going strong. And it continued to brief me almost exclusively as a junior and senior for twenty-nine years.

When I took my place in the courthouse on that day in January 1947 my heart sank. I could see little future for myself when I looked at the array of counsel. There was Thomas J. Connolly, Christopher Micks, John Willie O'Connor, Seamus Henchy, Charlie Conroy, John Durkan and Kevin Kenny. Naturally my wonder was how could I possibly survive among this galaxy of experience and talent. But fate played a big part then. Connolly, Kenny and Micks took silk, thereby reducing three very serious hurdles, and when the Government changed in 1948 I played some small part in getting Charlie Conroy out of my way onto the Circuit Court bench. Later John Durkan also moved to the bench, in about 1950 I think.

The way was clear thereafter. Or at least clearer.

* * * *

In the Circuit Court, as indeed in the High Court, there is a practice that when a witness, be he plaintiff, defendant or a supporting witness for either side, is too ill to attend court, the presiding judge appoints what's called a 'commissioner'. The commissioner is usually the newest recruit to the circuit, there are two guineas in it for him, and at that stage anything is a help.

The newest recruit to the circuit at that time was a charming fellow called Frank Shields, a son of the late Vincent Shields of Loughrea. Frank is now in Kenya and, I am told, doing extremely well.

I was very friendly with Frank and also fascinated by him. He was a sort of pre-period character, dressed in the style of the early 1900s maybe even before that. He spoke extremely well by reason of the expensive Jesuit education he had had. In any event Frank was appointed commissioner and his style certainly was different. He carried a bottle of ink and a nibbed pen which he produced extravagantly, and the uncorking of the bottle was always a great piece of showmanship.

We had to go out to a village called Glengowla, about five miles on the Clifden side of Oughterard. It was then a picturesque village of thatched cottages. I was attempting to set aside a deed made by the father of the house in favour of his son, made in the absence of the mother while she was visiting her own people. When she heard about it she got a solicitor out and the proceedings started.

When we arrived at the house the plaintiff (the father) was in bed in a smallish bedroom.

The only place that Frank Shields could use as a table or desk was an American trunk with serrated edges. There were strips of wood on the top, providing a very uneven surface for his notebook and a very unsafe place for his bottle of ink.

We started off when the commissioner was ready and I asked a few preliminary questions from the man in the bed; eventually I said to him: 'What age are you?' and he said: 'I'll be 86 coming MacDara's Day.'

I looked at Frank who had the pen poised in mid-air, looking at me questioningly. 'I beg your pardon, Pat' he said 'Did he say Derby Day?' Obviously MacDara didn't rank high as a saint in Jesuit halls.

* * * *

I recall one morning getting a telephone call from the late Paddy McEllin of Claremorris to know if I would appear for a client in the Castlebar Criminal Court on the following Tuesday week. Before accepting the brief I asked what the charges were, only to be told that there was a litany of motor offences, including manslaughter, drunken driving and dangerous driving. 'You probably read about it in the papers' Paddy MacEllin told me. 'The client in question is a member of the travelling classes and he was driving seven or eight of his brethren, visiting camps on the day before Christmas Eve, saying goodbye. They had one more camp to visit and they went over a level crossing and were hit by a train.'

'Oh' said I 'that's where there were seven or eight people killed.'

He said: 'Yes.'

I said: 'Tell that fellow to jump into the dock, and plead guilty straight away, and not to be wasting money.' I felt there was no point in wasting their money in bringing me down to act in a case where there was no hope whatsoever.

'Well,' said Paddy, 'they asked for you especially.'

'Why do they want me?'

'Well he said that you appeared for his aunt on a murder charge and you got her off.'

'Fair enough, I'll be there'.

I told them my fee which was quite high at the time and I went to Castlebar, saw my client for a minute or two, and told him not to hold out any great hopes.

We went into the court. I couldn't ask any of the witnesses a single question and the invariable remark from me was: 'No questions, My Lord.' That is until the last witness came up. He was the train driver and when he had given evidence, Judge Durkan said to me: 'I suppose you have no questions?'

'Well, I might.'

So I got up and I asked him what was the weight of the train. The judge intervened and asked of what relevance that was.

I said: 'I propose to make it relevant.'

'Very good' said the judge, 'carry on.' The driver then recited the weight of the train, having first enquired whether I wanted the weight of the engine or the rolling stock. So I invited him to give the two, so that we could add them, and it totalled 133 tons.

Then I asked him if the train had had a warning device and a braking system. His replies were in the affirmative so I asked him what speed he was doing. He said between 60 - 70 m.p.h. So I said: 'Here you are, hurtling 133 tons along the railway line from Westport to Castlebar – did you see the Morris Minor approach the level crossing?' 'I did.'

'Did you sound a warning?'

'No.'

'Did you slow down?'

'No.'

Then I paused and looked at the jury and said: 'Huh, I wonder who should be in the dock?' and sat down.

By this time the judge was quite enraged, and looked it. He said to me: 'Do you want to address the jury?' I said that I did, and I dealt at length with the reckless hurtling of this 133 ton vehicle, without warning, slowing down, or any signalling to other vehicles. I said that under the circumstances, the most my young client could be guilty of was careless driving and sat down.

The judge then charged them and informed them in quite strong language that my client could be guilty of several other things as well.

The jury retired about lunch time. We came back and the jury returned verdicts of 'not guilty' on everything except careless driving.

The judge did a thing I never heard him do before. He said to the jury: 'Gentlemen, I don't agree with your verdict but I have to accept it'.

At that time the maximum punishment for careless driving was a £10 fine and a suitable disqualification from driving. Whereupon the judge imposed the fine of £10 and disqualified my client from driving for five years.

I stood up rather solemnly, with tongue-in-both-cheeks, and said: 'I wish to make an application, My Lord.' Judge Durkan asked what kind of an application did I want to make.

'I want to apply for leave to appeal to the Court of Criminal Appeal.'

'For what possible reason?'

'Against severity of sentence. Five years disqualification is not in my view a proper punishment for a verdict of careless driving. It's excessive.'

'In my view it's not. I refuse your application.'

So the court closed and we left and my little client came over to me and said: 'Sir could I shake your hand?'

I said: 'Certainly.'

My client said: ' Sure I knew you'd save me, when you saved my aunt.' Incidentally, he was one of the only two clients in my whole career who said to me: 'Did I give you enough money ?'

I said: 'You did; you gave me what I asked and that's enough.'

He then invoked all the blessings of God and his Virgin Mother on me, and thanked me and stated how delighted he was that he didn't have to go to jail, because people from that part of the world didn't like jail.

He said goodbye to me again amidst further blessings, walked out the door of the Castlebar courthouse, sat into a new Morris Minor van and drove away.

I never told that story until Judge Durkan retired, otherwise he'd have got the Guards to bring him in. In fact when I did tell Judge Durkan the story later he laughed, but by this time he had mellowed greatly. I know to my knowledge that he did later describe me to other colleagues as 'a menace appearing for defendants in the Criminal Courts.' That did not displease me greatly.

* * * *

Another case I recall involved Eamon Gallagher of Rochford Gallagher in Tubbercurry. His letter to me simply said: 'I enclose a brief on behalf of the accused. He said he did what he is charged with but that he won't plead guilty. Do the best you can.'

The facts of the case were fairly straightforward. The accused was an elderly bachelor farmer, living in a new house on the family holding. In the family home, also living alone, was another elderly bachelor brother. My client, having discovered that his brother was 'keeping company' with a widow of some ill repute in the locality, had set fire to the family bed in the old family home. The fire had spread and damage had been done to one of the rafters in the kitchen. The fire wasn't particularly serious but nonetheless he was charged with arson.

When I asked my client why he did it he told me: 'It was in that bed we were all made... It was in that bed that we were all born... and I wasn't going to let this woman into that bed with my brother, as I heard he was going to marry her.'

Clearly he was determined to defend the memory of his parents and the honour of the family bed against a woman he felt to be unworthy.

This was the first and indeed the only case in which I drew upon whatever classical learning I had, because here clearly was the theme of Sophocles' *Antigone*. On the strength of that I persuaded my client that he should plead guilty, and that he would go home on the first bus after the court, a free man.

This was a bit offhand of me in the light of subsequent events.

We went in. He pleaded guilty. The police spoke in his favour. A clergyman spoke in his favour. In fact, there was so much said in his favour that one wondered why he was charged with anything at all. And then I addressed the court, relying heavily upon the theme of Sophocles' *Antigone* and on all my ancient classical learning. I said: 'My Lord, this case is the recurrence of a theme that has excited dramatists since the time of Sophocles. This is the story of Antigone repeated almost identically; the clash between one's duty to the dead and the law of the land.'

I was not however bargaining on the fact that the judge, the late Charlie Conroy was a graduate in Economics, an expert in Railway Law and knew nothing about the Humanities. So when I finished he shoved his glasses up his nose, looked at the accused and said: 'I hope every son doesn't show his regard for his deceased parents in this manner. I sentence you to nine calendar months with hard labour.'

I was stuck to the seat and so indeed was my client. I was on my way to see him, to offer such consolation as I could when the judge's crier called me and told me that Judge Conroy wanted to see me.

I went back into the judge's room and he said: 'Send in a petition, I'll recommend that he be released in two or three months.' I said: 'I'll do no such thing. You might be an expert in Economics and in Railway Law but you know nothing about the Humanities and you are not touched by them.'

I'm leaving out all the expletives which enlivened that particular exchange on both sides.

I went and saw my man and he said: 'Well, I had faith in you once.' I said: 'Well have faith in me again. You'll be on the bus home from Sligo jail tomorrow evening. Have faith in me.'

This case was the only criminal case in Castlebar that day, so by next morning I was back in Dublin and at an early hour I went into the office of my old and good friend, General Sean MacEoin, the blacksmith of Ballinalee, who was now Minister for Justice. I told him my story and he said: 'Well, it would be usual to refer that to the judge' and I said: 'Yes and that's why I am here to stop you, because I know what he'll recommend which would be two or three months.'

' What do you want me to do?'

'I want you to ring Sligo jail and tell the Governor to send that decent man home by the very next bus.'

So after a good deal of persuasion the Minister did make the phone call. I heard him do it. And then I sat on, telling stories, reminding him of various meetings we had addressed in various parts of the country.

Eventually MacEoin looked at his watch and said: 'Sonny, it's nearly 1 o'clock, what are you staying on for?'

'I'll tell you. It's now an hour and a half since you rang the jail. My client is on his way home now to Charlestown or at least he's at the bus stop. You see, I'd be inclined not to trust you anymore than I trust Conroy, because after I left, you could easily cancel the call.'

'Ah you blackguard' he said. 'Off with you now.'

My client arrived home that evening and I felt that justice had been done. But in addition I wanted to be fair to my friend Sophocles, who made the theme of that case so prominent in Classical Literature.

* * * *

Much has been written about the Irish being particularly litigious, but they're not as litigious as they used to be. Land rows, have, in the main, gone. In fact the craving for land seems to have gone altogether. When I first started in practice, the title action was a regular feature of every Circuit Court. People were fighting over two square yards of a little path or kesh, or a path to a well, or a mass path, or setting aside deeds.

Judge John Durkan had no difficulty in setting aside deeds but he treated them as wills. Mind you, he was well before his time if one examines the Succession Act of 1961 where the legislation virtually makes the will for you in spite of yourself. The old days of cutting the wife off without a shilling, or threatening that if she remarried she would have to give up her life tenancy, that kind of thing is all gone. Land, to a certain extent, has been devalued and there's also a loss of interest and a loss of pride in the land. I remember when farmers used to gather in a small village at home in Mayo when a reek of hay would be put in, or stacks of oats put up and trimmed, and the way they talked about it noting that a wisp here or a wisp there was out – they always took pride. It was pride of workmanship.

The fellows that beat and battered each other over keshes or paths weren't really interested in land. They were just greedy. Well that type of greed is no longer around. In some ways it would be small beer to the type of greed we see today – especially of the corporate variety.

* * * *

Since the days of the Locke's Whiskey Tribunal I have regarded tribunals as a white-washing process, set up for that purpose. I was present every day as a junior counsel, devilling with Charlie Conroy at the Locke's Tribunal and the findings left me aghast when I looked at the notes of evidence I had taken down. So I haven't much faith in tribunals. They arrive at the truth but I think they fail, by and large, to state what the truth is. And if you look at the Locke's Tribunal and look at all the protagonists in both the judiciary and police, you will see that they were all rewarded afterwards.

I believe the findings of the Locke Tribunal were just as significant as the arrival of Sean McBride's Clann na Poblachta in breaking the Fianna Fáil Government of 1948. I think the Irish people were shocked by the findings of that tribunal and that it contributed to the drop in the Government vote. That vote didn't go straight to Fine Gael. It went the new avenue of Clann na Poblachta and Clann na Talmhan, although that party was then coming to the end of its run. I always thought that people who went into these smaller parties, rather than straight across to Fine Gael or Fianna Fáil, were like the people who did their Easter duty in another parish.

* * * *

Barristers, like judges, have their own particular strengths and weaknesses. You get to know your colleagues very quickly and very thoroughly on Circuit. A camaraderie builds up, and a stranger, even a 'big name' stranger can find the going tough enough. Indeed, being a big Dublin 'name' can often be a disadvantage. I was not the first – and won't be the last – barrister to take full advantage of being a countryman and using my knowledge of the country mentality when pitted against the Dublin 'heavies'.

I recall one day Paddy McKenzie, recently retired as a High Court Judge, addressing a jury. He dealt very little with the case but warned the jury against me, saying that I was an eighteenth century gentleman, full of blarney and palaver. When it came to my turn to close the case to the same jury, I said: 'While Mr McKenzie has said many things about me, there's one thing he hasn't said and it is a thing of which I am most proud – I'm a countryman like you. I don't come from the highly valued slopes of Killiney on behalf of some financial institution who is not the real client.'

I remember getting a great verdict that day.

James Fitzgerald-Kenny was a dab hand at putting down counsel who came from Dublin. He could do it effortlessly, simply by describing them to a country jury as 'from Dublin'. So often, it was simply a question of timing.

I remember a very famous defamation action when Fitzgerald-Kenny was leading me and the initial letter from the defendant's solicitor said that their instructions were 'strenuously to defend.'

Fitzgerald-Kenny put down the letter, looked at the jury and said: 'And here gentlemen, strenuously to defend, is Mr Ernest Wood from Dublin.' I was sitting beside Ernest and I said: 'That's you finished.'

'I know' said Ernest, yet we won that particular action against all the odds.

Ernest Wood was a great character. He had, I think, the most incisive and caustic use of the English language I've ever heard. I recall one case in which he featured, which took place when I was reading for the Bar. I had gone to listen to this case because my inspiration for law, Charles Wyse Power was sitting in Dublin.

It was a singular kind of case. A lady was charged, under the Larcency Act of 1916, with stealing £500 from a friend of hers. The purpose for which the £500 was intended illustrated a quite extraordinary affair. A gentleman from somewhere in Eastern Europe had arrived in the country and his method of making a living was quite original. He spread the word that he was destined to become the father of the Messiah for the Second Coming. He was prepared to 'oblige' any lady who saw her destiny as being the mother of the new Messiah, and his fee for providing this service was £500. There was, of course, no charge against the man – he was merely a witness, but I remember Ernest Wood describing him as 'The most miserable piece of human wreckage that the tide of war ever wafted to any shore.'

Ernest's client was acquitted, but I did notice recently that an Irish authoress described that particular case very inaccurately when she said that the man who was alleging that he would be the father of the Messiah got off scot free. He was, as I said never charged with anything. He was merely a witness.

Ernest Wood was absolutely great. He went into a bar one day and was offered a glass of champagne from a strange source, a lawyer not known to pass around drink too freely. And he had a second and a third glass and couldn't understand the reason for this largesse. He later found out that this man was celebrating his appointment to the judiciary but in fact, his information was wrong. He hadn't been appointed, and Ernest Wood telling the story afterwards described it as 'The Feast of the Passover.'

* * * *

I had a very serious set-back in 1949, just when my practice was picking up. I noticed one day a rather stinging pain when I was shaving the right-hand side of my face. I told Declan Quigley about it. Declan took a pencil out of his pocket and lifted the hair on my head and said: 'There are spots, bald spots under your hair.' So I immediately repaired to a doctor friend of mine who told me that she knew very little about skin trouble but recommended me to a colleague in Galway.

I went to him and told him that my suspicion was that this had happened through using a brushless shaving cream called 'Morning Pride'. He, not slow on the uptake, gave me the definition of what was wrong with me. He called it 'Chemical Depilation'.

I went straight to a solicitor who wrote to the manufacturers of 'Morning Pride.' They replied, saying that they would strenuously defend any proceedings we cared to take. The following weekend we went down to Mayo and called to some solicitor friends of mine, the Hannons in Foxford and Mrs Hannon said to me: 'George Hewson, the chemist in Ballina, has the cure for that.'

So I went to see George Hewson on the Monday morning. George, a very brilliant man, had, in fact, invented the puncture-proof bicycle tube (when the air went down through reason of a puncture, all you did was turn your bicycle upside down, spin the wheel, and whatever fluid was in the tube filled up the gash or pinhole). I believe Dunlops bought it off him, in case it would be a success, and nobody has heard of it since. But George gave me a set of towels and bottles of astringents and ointments of all kinds, with the necessary instructions.

He told me that it would take some months for the hair to come back, but not to worry, that it would come back and it would come back in regular shape, not piebald.

The following Wednesday I went to Belmullet Circuit Court. When the court was over I called at the local branch of the National Bank and met the wife of the bank manager, Mrs McCormack, who told me that she had a very sore toe, I said: 'I'm not too concerned about your toe, look at my head.'

At this time the beard was no longer growing on my face, the only survivor was the family coat of arms, my eyebrows. And she said: 'I have the very thing that'll cure you', and she produced a large jar with stuff the same colour as mustard, and applied it to my head – she said she had been a nurse herself, and I accepted that she knew what she was doing. She said: 'Your hair will grow in three days.'

I went back to Ballina that night, stayed in the Moy Hotel, and the following morning I was appalled to see the pillowcases and sheets purple from this particular stuff. I knew I would probably get into trouble with the hotel people for this, so I confessed. While I was confessing I decided on another thing – to go back to George Hewson and confess what had been done in Belmullet. He looked at me through his rimless glasses and trained on me the most piercing pair of penetrating eyes I have ever seen. He said: 'You spent a long time at school, going to secondary school, university, law school and you have had a lot of experience. Tell me, did you ever have a child?' I looked at him stupidly I suppose and said: 'No.'

'Well now,' he said, 'when you get back to Dublin tonight wash that damn stuff out of your hair. It's not going to do you any good. It's a different kind of ointment altogether. It's for post-natal alopecia in women.'

I went back to Dublin and the very dear landlady with whom I was staying in Sandymount put on her rubber gloves and washed my hair. When I eventually looked there was nothing left but eyebrows. I spent a very sleepless night and in my humiliation considered departing from Mayo and leaving the Bar generally. I felt I would not be recognised and people would pass me by.

The mane had gone and even my wig was now too big for me. However, through the help of a seamstress I got a piece of elastic put in and around the wig so it fitted on the bare bald head. It took almost a year for the hair to return to normal but it did come back and for that I shall always be grateful.

We didn't pursue 'Morning Pride' because of what George Hewson told me. He had given me a great description of this particular disease if, I suppose, you could call it that. Alopecia is where the oil ducts fail and the hair breaks off. It doesn't come off by the root – the root is still there, and his treatment stimulated the root and created fresh oil ducts. He told me that every single hair has an oil duct between the inner and outer skin, and when the oil duct fails the hair falls out. He said it was due, probably, to some kind of nervous trouble, which in my case he rather unkindly attributed to 'giving drink up suddenly, and never being treated for shock after motor accidents' – my driving had never been great.

* * * *

Before I was called to the Bar there was a very curious incident in Bangor Erris Garda Station. At that time, under the health regulations or legislation, it was necessary that a person about to be committed to a mental hospital would have to have two peace commissioners, a doctor, and the police in attendance. Among the particular forms which had to be filled, there was one in which the peace commissioners had to certify the fee of one guinea for the doctor.

As I mentioned earlier, my father (one of the peace commissioners) and the doctor were extremely friendly and my father always exercised the right, which was there in brackets, which said: 'In exceptional cases a fee of two guineas may be recommended'. In this case, as was his usual practice, my father recommended the fee of two guineas. The form was then handed over to the other peace commissioner (who didn't particularly like the doctor) and he changed the two guineas back to one guinea.

The form was then handed to the doctor to sign. When he saw the changed fee he tore the form up and made for the peace commissioner grabbing him by the throat. Suddenly they were all sprawling on the floor, doctor, peace commissioners, guards, the lot. Over all the din could be heard the voice of the man about to be committed, saying: 'For God's sake men, would ye have sense. I'm the cause of all this.'

You'd wonder who should have committed whom.

* * * *

One day early in my career I was sitting in the Law Library with what was, in those days, always a problem because after three years of law lectures one knew so little about practicing, precedence or procedural drafting. I had a difficult problem about a will, and, in frustration, I looked up and there was a little man with glasses smiling at me. He said: 'Are you in trouble?' and I said: 'Yes'. I then told him what my trouble was and he walked away, to my disgust, because that was very unlike what happens in the library. Help is always forthcomimg. However, in a few minutes he was back with three books, two volumes of Jarman on *Wills*, and Maxwell's *Probate Practice*. Setting them down in front of me he said: 'The answer is in them. When you find it, tell me.'

That was Charlie Casey, later to become Attorney General and High Court judge. He was a really lovely man. He was then a fellow barrister and a silk, and extremely good.

* * * *

The only time that I ever appeared to mislay papers happened when I was staying in the Imperial Hotel in Galway and a solicitor came in with a brief file. He didn't give it to the girl at the reception desk but went upstairs to my room and threw it on my bed. At that time there was a very decent head porter, a man called Tommy Morrissey, who looked after me like you would look after a rare piece of Beleek and he invariably unpacked and packed my bag.

A couple of months later I got a letter from the solicitor who had thrown this brief on my bed, wanting to know what I was doing about it. We were running out of time, he said. (The Public Authorities Protection Act at that time made it necessary to bring action within six months of the cause of complaint).

I wrote back and said I never had papers of any such case. The solicitor wrote back and said it was left in my bedroom. Now the old suitcase that I used was never fully emptied. Sometime later, but after the six months had elapsed I found the file in the bottom of the suitcase, carefully tucked away by poor Tommy Morrissey.

Charlie Casey was Attorney General at the time and I went to him in the Law Library and told him my story. He said: ' How much do you want?' and I said: ' Well, it would be close to the £300 which was the Circuit Court Jurisdiction at that time. He said: ' Write me a letter setting all that out.' I did, and he gave £290 and costs but *ex gratia* I didn't care whether it was *ex gratia* or not, as long as I got it. I never forgot the name of that case – *Fahy versus the Minister for Finance*, a running down action where an army lorry knocked this man down but didn't cause him an awful lot of injury, otherwise he'd have gone to the High Court.

* * * *

I was a junior in the first jury action in Galway when the High Court began the practice of hearing jury actions in the country towns. It was an ordinary motor accident case – *Kelly versus Mitchell*, I was for the plaintiff and the jury awarded us £1,500 but, in the course of their deliberation, they came back with a question as to what would happen about costs. The judge properly informed them that costs weren't any of their business, and that he would deal with them. So they went out and came back with their verdict of £1,500. It was promptly appealed and when it reached the Supreme Court, the award was considered excessive and the case was sent back for re-trial.

In the second trial the same question was asked by the foreman of the jury about costs, and the jury got the same instructions from the judge. The jurors went out again and increased the decree to £2,000. I was talking to one of them afterwards and he said the reason for their increased decree to £2,000 was that they felt the plaintiff would have to pay the costs.

Another appeal resulted and Tommy Connolly was leading me in this. We were about to go into court when the late Billy Fitzgerald who was acting for the defence said to me: 'We'll give you the original £1,500 and the costs of the two trials, but you'll have to go back to the Supreme Court.

So I rang my solicitor in Galway and told him the story and he said: 'Grab it'. We did, and that was the end of that.

* * * *

I recall another appeal from Galway and, curiously enough, it was Billy Fitzgerald who appealed it too. He had a huge insurance practice and, as the late John Kenny said to me one day, he was amazed at a man of the brilliance of Billy Fitzgerald tying himself to the bumpers of cars. Anyway, I was in the Supreme Court trying to uphold a verdict of £4,000 for a girl from Galway who had been injured in a car crash – a lot of money in those days.

Billy Fitzgerald had lodged £3,000 in court, and as we had beaten the lodgement in Galway, everything was alright. But when I was about to finish my argument before the Supreme Court, Cearbhall O' Dalaigh, with his customary politeness, almost apologetically, asked me if I would mind if the Supreme Court saw this girl themselves. Such a request was unusual and I objected strenuously.

Beetroot-red with anger, Cecil Lavery, one of the members of the Supreme Court nearly came over the bench to devour me with a simple incisive query: 'Why?' I said: 'Well, I'm not prepared to substitute twelve good Galway men and true for five urban dwellers.'

The other four judges laughed, but Lavery sat back and looked hurt. Eventually the suggestion from Cearbhall O'Dalaigh was put to the client and she came up.

I always thought it was a very farcical performance. I walked in with her to the boardroom of the Supreme Court. The five judges were sitting there. No word was spoken. I turned her right and I turned her left and full forward.

They all had a look and went out. There wasn't a word spoken the whole time. They eventually gave a three-two judgement in my favour. The younger members of the bench were for me, Lavery and Kingsmill-Moore were against me. But they were of the age not to be influenced by any girl's beauty being impaired.

* * * *

The Circuit-going barristers owe a great debt to what were known as the 'Bar Hotels' where we stayed. They were kind, they were not particular whether you paid your bill after a bad circuit or not, but we always finished up not owing them anything. For instance, in the Imperial Hotel in Galway, there was a tremendous woman whom we all knew as 'Auntie Kelly'. She was the aunt of the ultimate owner of the hotel, Angela Bailey, later Angela Allen. In Castlebar we went to the Pelleys in the Imperial Hotel. They couldn't be kinder or more helpful. We also spent one night in Westport, four times a year, where we stayed in Jeffers' Hotel. John Jeffers, long since gone, was a decent man. And of course you couldn't beat the McMonagles in both the Moy and Imperial Hotels in Ballina.

The curious things about circuit towns was that one did not get to know many people, apart from the solicitors. The hotels were usually quite near the courthouses and our socialising was usually fairly self-contained. In Galway I had certain visiting houses: Kennedys was one of them, the Minahans in Nun's Island (they were nieces of the late Fr Tom Fahy, my old professor in Galway) and I would visit the

Costelloes and the Gavins. In Castlebar, I had two or three visiting houses: Michael Geraghty's, Ann Daly's in Spencer Street and Thorntons', the State solicitors place. He had a wonderful wife. I don't know what her real first name was but Alfred Thornton always called her 'Bird'. She too had a cure for me during my bout of alopecia. In her case when I told her about my baldness she said to me: 'God be with James O'Brien from Claremorris. He was a vet, and he had a bottle for curing mange in horses.' It was just as well that I didn't try this one out too. And of course in Ballina I enjoyed the friendship and hospitability of the Hastings, Garveys and Waters.

When the day's hearing was over there was always a social element to being on circuit, but there was never any discussion about cases with the judge. In general, in fact the judges stayed apart. I used to meet Charles Wyse Power by myself but we never discussed cases although his name evokes memories of one very funny case which occurred in Galway. It involved some aspect of Scottish Law and I remember that Seamus Henchy was on the other side opposite me. Wyse Power adjourned the case to Ballina on the following Monday.

Later Wyse Power asked me had I any drafting paper. I said I hadn't but I had a new notebook which I hadn't used. He said: 'That will do. I suppose you know what I want it for?' 'Well, I don't, M'Lord,' I said (we hadn't dropped to simple 'judge' at that time). He said: 'I have to reserve judgement on that damned Scottish Law case.' So I gave him the notebook.

Seamus Henchy who had ceased practicing in Mayo at that time arrived in Ballina from Dublin on the Monday morning with an armful of books. Wyse Power ignored him, delivered the judgement and to my embarrassment, handed down to the County Registrar my notebook saying: 'That's Mr Lindsay's notebook.' There was only one word on it – 'Draft.'

Also on the subject of the Circuit, I have to say that the best briefs in my time were provided by the firms of Dillon-Leetch in Ballyhaunis and F.J. Gearty of Longford. Both offices paid promptly.

* * * *

At the beginning of my increase in practice in the High Court I came to a decision that I would never ask a judge to recall a jury; 'To put them right' as they used to say, on certain matters in which counsel would be alleging that he had misdirected himself, whether in law or in fact.

I recall vividly what Judge Charles Wyse Power said to me one evening: 'Lindsay, remember this. Facial expressions, stressing your words, inflections of the voice do not appear on the note and are of very little use to you in the Court of Criminal Appeal.'

One such incident did occur in the Court of Criminal Appeal during a murder trial. I was asked by a member of that court, the late Judge John Kenny: 'Why didn't you ask the judge to recall the jury and deal with this matter?' 'I do not follow that practice. I do not believe in it on the simple basis that one cannot unring a rung bell.' The Court of Criminal Appeal sat back and pressed me no further on the subject. In the event my appeal was allowed.

I had faith, great faith, and still have in the Court of Criminal Appeal because it judges independently, acts independently and operates the system extremely well.

Indeed the Supreme Court operates on much the same basis and I am glad to note at this stage of writing that there are such men on the Supreme Court now, like Niall McCarthy and Seamus Egan who can always be relied upon as the protectors of the people's right to know. Just as I review these very words, news comes in of the death of Niall McCarthy. I will not change them because I believe that Niall's legacy to that Court will be a lasting one. He was stylish. He was substantial and he was humane with a remarkable if surprising common touch.

In my personal experience and I hasten to stress personal, I have found every Garda witness, from the ranks to Chief Superintendent, human and always willing to agree that a 'mistake' could have been made. By 'mistake' I mean that a measurement might be wrong, that an identification might not be quite correct. Of course, during a trial once a police witness replies that there could be the possibility of a mistake, defending counsel has immediately established a doubt to the benefit of which he is entitled. I have found the police good in this regard and I have worked both with them and against them. I can truthfully say that I didn't lose friends in the police as a result of cross-examination, however harsh.

I would extend that to forensic evidence, although I never came across this so called 'Griess test'. I can only speak of my own personal experience and I never came across a statement that was altered. I do, however, recall one statement that was misread in court when I was guilty of negligence.

It was a murder trial in which the question of a 'suicide pact' arose and the policeman in question, now a retired former Assistant Commissioner, John Paul McMahon, read out the statement which I had in front of me. Mr McMahon read as follows: '*He* poured the sherry and *I* put in the strychnine.' That case was coming up for its third trial when, the night before, I re-read the brief. Having done so, I went up to Green Street the following morning, before the trial started and I said to the policeman concerned: 'John, you have been misreading this statement and I have been equally negligent in not correcting you.' So he said: 'What have I being doing?'
'Read the last part'. He read it. 'My God, you're right.'

It should have been: '*I* poured the sherry and *he* put in the strychnine.' That was a serious mistake on the part both of a Chief

Superintendent of the Guards and of a Senior Counsel for the defence. It was put right during the third trial in which the accused was acquitted.

* * * *

I was appointed Master of the High Court by the Government of Liam Cosgrave, with effect from 1 November 1975 – the Feast of All Saints – the exact anniversary of the day I had been called to the Bar 29 years earlier.

Those who know me would say that my contacts with the saints could hardly be great. Let's just call it coincidence.

When I took up my position as Master of the High Court the court sat on Tuesday, Thursday and Friday. I decided that there was a need to make use of Wednesday. So I decided to transfer all Marital Law and anything in relation to Marital Law to Wednesday. It was a more private day.

Any day that I worked after lunch-time as Master was rare. I got through things fast, and I attributed the speed with which I was able to turn over an awful lot of work to the honesty and integrity of the people appearing before me. There were very few people – I can think of only one – whose word I would not take. And generally if you asked: 'Are your proofs in order?' or 'Are your papers in order?' and the answer was 'Yes', then you knew you could believe what you were told. 'Very good,' I would say, 'take your order.' That was it.

One of the Senior Registrars said to me one day: 'Do you know that you are the administrative head of the Central Office?'

'No, I didn't know.'

'You are, and you should drop in now and again.'

'Well,' I said, 'I certainly will not.'

'Why?'

'Look,' I said, 'whenever I wanted a precedent, anything in practice or procedure, or a precedence for a certain kind of defence, or a statement of claim, I went to the most junior fellow in the Central Office and he gave it to me accurately. Now, I'm not going to go in now and do the boss bit over fellows who have helped me over many years.'

I never went into the Central Office.

* * * *

During my time as Master I met with great loyalty from barristers, from solicitors, even solicitors' apprentices. Of course, no account would be complete without expressing my gratitude to my tipstaff, Liam Bates, who could not have been more loyal or more faithful. I had too, the great privilege of having two of my children who are involved in the legal profession, appear in front of me – Alison, as a barrister and John as a solicitor – and I think they were probably the most frightened people to ever appear before me. They had a good idea of my capability to erupt.

* * * *

I think the introduction of Family Courts was a good thing, but I also think that the people in charge of the Family Court should be selected after a fine-combing examination. The Family Court is a court governed by common sense, by a sense of humanity, by consideration of all the difficulties that can occur, by being able to recognise the good points of each side and to do justice in a fair-play kind of way. Not technical justice: common sense, human justice.

Before the Family Court you would have to go to the High Court for an annulment.

Long before I went to the Bar, I recall the case of a man who married, because his wife-to-be told him she was pregnant. She wasn't, but it took 20 years to get the annulment from Rome. And it took another five to get it to the High Court.

The whole thing was daft. The Family Courts have now become nice and approachable and for the most part, not too expensive. They allow marriage break-ups to be exposed and resolved. There has always been marital breakdown in this country but it was hidden or cloaked-over in pretence. People were ashamed to admit such things years ago. The Family Courts have done good in that they have brought things out into the open, and maybe it's on the way towards persuading the clergy not to be so rigorous in their attitude to divorce and annulment.

I support divorce, but I would make it difficult to get. It would have to be genuine breakdown. There would have to be a total absence of consensus, as between the parties. After all, marriage is a contract, and if the parties are not *ad idem* then there is no contract. You can have that from the very beginning, particularly with young people.

Divorce should never have been a constitutional provision, of course. It wasn't in the old 1922 Constitution. It should never have been in the new one either. But, if divorce did become lawful in this country, I don't think you'd have the flood-gates open or many people applying, largely because there aren't that many people in this country who can afford alimony and also start another family.

In fact, it might be a good thing for the social fabric of the country, if divorce were there to be availed of. I think many would be agreeably surprised by the small number of people who would make use of it.

* * * *

Looking back at my life at the bar I can only say that I enjoyed every bit of it. Mind you it was hard work. Not too bad in the first years because, though I didn't have much work, I managed to survive.

I recall that on 3 November 1946 I called to see the local bank manager in Belmullet, Mr Jim McCormack with a view to arranging a little supply of what was then called an overdraft. But he posed a question that absolutely stunned me: 'Have you any collateral?'

I didn't know what 'collateral' meant. He then explained it to me and we took out an insurance policy on my life for some miserable sum like a £1,000, but that was collateral enough for him and he looked after me during my lean years.

He was a very decent man and despite my attitude to banks I have met some very decent managers.

However, the more decent the bank manager the more trouble he can land you in. I remember that Jim McCormack, having nearly destroyed me through his generous lending, told me it would be better if I transferred to College Green, he told me, with great solicitude that the Fine Gael fellows did very well in there. His real purpose however was to get rid of me.

I went to College Green and there I met another very decent man, the now deceased Jimmy Hayes. Jimmy would never write you a letter, or ring you at home. He would ring me at the Law Library and say: 'Come in, come in. We are in terrible trouble.' He would never say: ' *You* are in terrible trouble.' So I would go in and he would say: 'Have you had your lunch?' 'No' I'd reply. 'We'll go out to the Moira and have a little bite.'

So we would go out to the Moira and have a liquid lunch. Then he would shove a piece of paper in front of me: 'There's an extra £500 for you now.'

I would walk out into the rarified air of College Green thinking I was £500 richer. I wasn't. I was £500 the poorer – but I spent it all the same.

Then I transferred to the Montrose branch where I met a very decent man, Jack Higgins. He was followed by a slightly harder gent called Michael Meaney, harder but nonetheless a very decent man. I always think of bank managers and insurance claims managers in relation to ethnic disputes. You can say: 'I hate such and such a race' and then you meet members of that race and they are charming fellows and decent people and good friends.

It is the 'institutions' I dislike. The institutions to me were robbers and grinders. Frequently the small man had no chance with them. I have seen banks suing people who shouldn't be sued at all.

I remember one day the wife of a man who owed the Bank of Ireland money was sued for the sum, because she was the registered owner of a nice little farm. But she had never had any part in the contract. I ruled against the Bank and gave her mighty expenses.

That was just one of the many cases where I made no apology for making life as difficult as possible for the institutions. In my time as Master, I saw myself as the protector of the lawful rights of the small man or woman against the banks, the insurance companies and, worst of all at times, the Revenue. The institutions could afford expensive lawyers, the small man was often on his own. Perhaps the best tribute I could get in this regard was to be told that some of the banks and insurance companies could not wait for me to retire, such was their antipathy to me. That pleased me greatly. I regarded it as proof that I was doing my job.

In fact that tribute was paid to me by Patrick McEntee when I retired as master of the High Court. I regard Paddy McEntee as probably the brightest man in the Law Library, which increased the pleasure of his remark that day.

Describing me as a lawyer and a classicist, Paddy said I was, sadly one of the rapidly declining race – a classicist lawyer. In that capacity I had taught members of the Bar that the world in which they had embarked as practitioners was not one bounded entirely by the stern realities of law. It also had other vistas – aspects of civilisation and culture which could be enjoyed side by side with their legal careers.

He said the principal characteristics of my tenure of office was the charm and humour I had brought to my duties. As Master, my office had been 'a bastion of freedom and protection for the small man'.

On that same occasion the then Attorney General, Peter Sutherland said I fell into the category of a 'real character in the Bar, of which there were very few left'. They all enjoyed my witticisms – especially if they were not at the receiving end of the barbs.

And Peter Sutherland added that there would be a mixed reaction from my colleagues at either being included or excluded from my memoirs when I came to write them.

Well, as you can see by now my memories dwell with great affection – and the odd barb – on former colleagues, past and happily still present.

Part III

Politics

Ifirst stood for election to the Dáil in 1937. I was still a student at University College Galway working for my MA when I was approached by Liam Burke, the then General Secretary of Fine Gael. Liam Burke had known me from the Ard Fheiseanna and because I already had something of a reputation as a public speaker.

In fact my first public speech was made at Maree Co. Galway, in the 1933 General Election when I spoke on behalf of two of the Cumann na nGaedhael candidates, Sean Broderick and Paddy Cawley. I spoke again during the 1934 local elections and in the subsequent Galway by-elections. The first of these was caused by the death in 1935 of Mairtin Mór McDonagh and then a year later we had the second by-election, caused this time by the tragic death of Patrick Hogan in a car crash. Patrick Hogan's loss was well-nigh irreparable. I was not very busy when Liam Burke's telegram reached me at UCG and I had no hesitation in accepting.

I had no illusions of how rough or tough the campaign was going to be. In some ways I was already a veteran and knew what to expect at public meetings – or at least I thought I did. I was prepared to be constructive and my early speeches in 1933 had much to say about the development of fisheries, the need to build more houses, to have proper sanitation and of course, the whole question of rural development. But of course all this constructive stuff went nowhere unless it was peppered with personal and political insults – and I quickly became a master of that art also.

I still remember that first meeting at Maree. It was after early Mass and the four Fine Gael speakers were Robert Jackson, a Commerce student at UCG, Chris Micks a barrister, Lord Hempel and myself. I was so nervous that the carrier on which I was standing was actually shaking.

Things improved at our second meeting which took place after a later Mass at Ballinderreen. It was after this bout of speaking that I began to discover for the first time that politics had its perks as well. Lord Hempel brought us back to his home, Tullira Castle, and gave us lunch. It was a great lunch by any standards but for a first year student it was a banquet. There were things there I had never seen before – for example, each guest had his own condiment set and for the first time I drank table wine (I had earlier tasted altar wine, but this was the real thing).

The following Sunday we spoke at Labane where the parish priest, Fr Considine was an irreconcilable republican and was not shy about showing his hostility to us. In fact his sermon at Mass consisted of a warning to his congregation not to listen to any speakers who had not been out in 1916 or 1922 – a bit hard on Micks, Jackson and myself considering how all of us were far too young at that time – but obviously aimed at Hempel. I have to say that Father Considine's attitude frightened us. It certainly frightened me as I wondered about the effect his inflammatory words might have on our audience. Hempel however was not perturbed and said he would go it alone.

I remember him still, tall, handsome and extremely able as he addressed that sullen meeting: 'My people, I wasn't out in 1916 or 1922 but I want to inform Fr Considine that I am more entitled to speak to you than he was to warn you not to listen to me. The reason I say this is were it not for the generosity of my uncle, Edward Martyn, there would be no church in Labane today.' He was lustily cheered but our votes in the ballot box did not reflect the applause.

In any event I accepted Liam Burke's invitation to run in North Mayo but when I arrived for the election campaign I was left under no illusion as to the appalling state of the party in the constituency. The party organisation was in chaos. There were no branches, no executive – no structure of any kind. The constituency boundaries had been altered in 1935 and this had added to the general confusion, though why it should have been so bad I don't know.

One of the outgoing TD's was Michael Davis, a well-dressed, wax-moustached merchant from Ballina, one of a family of merchant princes with shops in Ballina, Crossmolina and Killala, in the 'Golden Triangle' of good Mayo land. He had represented Mayo since 1927 and had been chairman of the Cumann na nGaedhael Parliamentary Party. He now felt it was time to stand down.

Another of the outgoing TD's was James Morrisroe, brother of the then Bishop of Achonry, a prelate incidentally who did not trouble to hide his political allegiances – even to the point of sending a telegram to Eoin O'Duffy in December 1933 after the courts had ordered his release from Arbour Hill following his arrest at Westport. That telegram I remember pulled no punches: 'Congratulations' it said, 'on victory of justice over shameless partisanship and contemptible tyranny.' I suppose in fairness if Fianna Fáil had its Fr Considine we had our Bishop Morrisroe. Anyway, by 1937 James Morrisroe was ill but he stayed in politics opting to run for the new Mayo South constituency, where in fact he was defeated and died shortly afterwards.

The result of all of this was that all three Fine Gael candidates in North Mayo were new. Patrick Browne from Crossmolina, Michael James O'Hara from Attymachugh and myself. It was, like all the elections at the time, a rough tough affair and meetings were rarely heard without interruptions and hecklers. This suited me because I would on occasion appoint my own hecklers to ask me the right questions. The Civil War was very much alive, but the main emphasis was on personalised abuse with little respect for the laws of slander – I cannot complain, I gave as good, if not better than I got.

I polled just under 2,000 votes and saved my deposit by three votes. Fianna Fáil had no difficulty in winning two of the three seats with their candidates P.J. Ruttledge and John Munnelly of Ballina. The single Fine Gael seat was won by Patrick Browne and the total Fine Gael vote was not more than 40 per cent. As I said, Fine Gael at that time in

Mayo was in chaos but more than that, it was family run and we had nothing like Fianna Fáil's organisational skills – which was our fault not theirs.

The main Fine Gael families in North Mayo were the Murphys of Ballina, the Brownes of Crossmolina, the O'Reillys of Belmullet and Jack O'Donaghue who owned the Royal Hotel, also in Belmullet. All of these families had money, 'old money' for the most part, and while they were generous they were not vote gatherers and their exclusivity undoubtedly weakened the popular appeal of the party. Nonetheless I owe them a great debt, as I do to some of the other stalwart Fine Gael families such as the O'Donnells of Mulrany, people who were as tough as they were loyal. In Achill there were the Lavelles, the O'Malleys, the Heeneys, the Mills, the Hogans and the McNamaras. My greatest supporter of all, Tony Chambers later to achieve nationwide fame in the 'Ballroom of Romance' and still going strong, had not yet arrived on the scene. He was to be vital to me in later elections.

After the 1937 election I went back to UCG and finished my MA. I left Galway in October for home, but around Christmas I was offered a job in Khartoum. My father advised me against it on the grounds that 'in a year or two the Mediterranean would be a hot spot.' I wrote to virtually every secondary school in Ireland looking for a job. I got only one reply – from Dr John Charles McQuaid, President of Blackrock College who wished me well on account of my high qualifications but unfortunately was unable to offer me a job. That was the beginning of a relationship with Dr McQuaid which later blossomed into a friendship. He was a man of fundamental values for whom I have always had a very high regard and a man whom I believe has been misrepresented in many of the things he did.

However, I was still in Mayo, unemployed, helping neighbours and doing some deep-sea fishing when the 1938 election was called. De Valera had lost his overall majority in the 1937 election and after a defeat on a minor issue in the Dáil he called a snap election in 1938. I was again approached to run, this time by local party stalwarts. This time I was under no illusion as to what my role was to be. My main function was to collect the number two votes in the Erris Peninsula for Patrick Browne. I was not particularly put out by this and enjoyed the campaign.

It was a quieter campaign. Already much of the steam and much of the bitterness of the Civil War era was going out of politics. Once again I enjoyed the electioneering. This time my vote was up by 1,000 votes and Browne held the single Fine Gael seat.

Once again Fine Gael had no organisation and we found ourselves at our usual disadvantage to Fianna Fáil who were both highly organised and had placed their people in key jobs all over the county, especially on the roadworks and indeed other types of patronage under the control of the county council.

After the 1938 election I went first to Cavan where I was not at all involved in politics and there then followed the hard, penurious years in Dublin in the 1940s. However my Fine Gael background did help me in that Liam Burke was able to get me work in Marino Technical College and Martin Gleeson who later became a great friend of mine, was also extremely helpful to me at that stage. It was through him that I got part-time teaching work and managed to survive.

When the 1943 election was called the Fine Gael organisation was in an even worse state. People were beginning to say that as soon as the Civil War generation died away so too would Fine Gael. I never accepted that and never will. So when the invitation came to stand once again in North Mayo I had no hesitation in accepting the challenge.

When I got back to Mayo I found that the local organisation was even worse than it had been five years earlier. In addition to the well-entrenched Fianna Fáil organisation, there was this time one other major difference and that was the emergence of Farmers candidates. Clann na Talmhan has not yet been formed but the Farmers movement, fuelled by the anger of the appalling conditions and shortages, was making great headway. From a local Fine Gael point of view what was even worse was the fact that two of the Farmers candidates, Niall McCormack from Lacken and Tommy O'Hara from Foxford were former Fine Gael Councillors.

It was a wartime election, quiet and uneventful. Because of the rationing of petrol most of the travelling was done on bicycles, and this in turn limited the number of public meetings we could have. More than that there was a scarcity of newsprint, the newspapers were but a pale shadow of what they had been and this meant very little coverage of the election. That in turn dampened down the campaign, and worked to the favour of the Government. On top of all of that was the fact that we were in the middle of a world war which the Government exploited to the full by stressing the danger of changing leadership at this crucial time.

My vote this time was down to its 1937 level, the bulk of the lost Fine Gael votes – about 10 per cent – going to the Farmers. My presence on the ticket was crucial however in helping Browne hold the Fine Gael seat. But the warning from the Farmers was loud and clear. In that same election in South Mayo, Fianna Fáil and Fine Gael each lost a seat to the Farmers.

I wasn't asked to run in 1944 – something which pleased me, given my state of penury. Though in fact the failure to ask me was instigated by Joe Leneghan of Belmullet, who saw a chance for himself. In the event, his vote was lower even than mine had been a year earlier, in spite of his being a full-time resident in the constituency (he had a pub in Belmullet) while I was an absentee.

By 1948 I was a practising barrister on the Western Circuit. By then Clann na Talmhan was well established and had made major inroads on the Fine Gael vote – it had also begun to erode the Fianna Fáil support as well. Clann na Poblachta had arrived on the scene also, led by Sean McBride and there were some, including *Time* magazine who spoke of him as Ireland's 'Man of Destiny' and saw Clann na Poblachta becoming the major opposition party, sweeping aside the increasingly feeble Fine Gael challenge. It's strange how some themes recur in Irish politics – they were later to say the same about the Progressive Democrats and we see where they are today.

I was on circuit in Galway when an approach was made to me to run. Leneghan was unwilling to stand and I have to say that I was not particularly enthusiastic either. However, I agreed and Brendan Allen, a son of Michael Allen who was a great benefactor of mine as a student in UCG, drove me to Ballinrobe. There, I was met by Pat Browne and rubber stamped as a candidate the day before nominations closed. I got my worst vote ever in that election – hardly surprising given the strong Clann na Poblachta presence, and the candidature of Michael Hefferon from my own area, running for that party. But my votes, which would have gone to Hefferon had I not stood, ensured that Browne held his seat, one of only 29 Fine Gael seats won in that election.

I have however one great memory of that 1948 election, or rather of its aftermath. There was no certainty that an Inter-Party Government could be put together or that de Valera could be ousted – indeed most Fianna Fáil people refused to even contemplate such a thing happening, including I believe de Valera himself. In any event the heavy speculation continued right up to the last minute.

I was out of Dublin, frustratingly out of touch on circuit in Galway, on the day the new Dáil met. I waited as long as I could in Galway to get the result of the election for Taoiseach, but I had to go to Dunmore for a consultation with a solicitor there, Ambrose Nestor.

I was going down the road to Tuam and I saw papal flags flying out of some houses and I said to myself, 'He's back again' the 'he' being de Valera. Then I continued on my journey and I met a fellow on a bicycle with his cap turned backways. He looked to me like a typical Fianna Fáil road ganger and he looked vicious and disappointed, and I thought, 'There's still hope.'

I drove into Tuam and I saw there the large physique of a man, a civic guard, who was standing on the footpath. I pulled in *diagonally* and lowered my window.

'Guard, is there any news from Dublin?'

'At ten past five this afternoon, Mr John Aloysius Costello was elected Taoiseach of this Country.'

I knew by the way he said it, that this really meant something to him and I said: 'Guard would you like a drink?'

'We'll have two.'

'Will you wait a minute, until I park this car?'

'Leave it where it is. We have freedom for the first time in sixteen years.'

We had more than one drink that day.

* * * *

My main interest during the 1948-1951 period was of course building up my Bar practice but I continued to be interested in politics and kept up contacts with those politicians in Dublin that I knew and I frequently went into the Dáil to listen to debates. I was also in the Fine Gael national organisation and was a member of the Standing Committee of the party.

When the election of 1951 came I considered running but in fact was not given the opportunity. Once again, Joe Leneghan jumped in and got the nomination, and once again he failed to make any real impact.

On the death of P. J. Ruttledge, the Fianna Fáil TD, in 1952 I was selected as the Fine Gael candidate for the ensuing by-election. Leneghan did not contest that convention. In fact when the convention was under way he came into the hall, looked around, and said: 'This place is packed' and walked out.

To say that it was 'packed' would be to seriously over-estimate our organisational ability at that time. It was in truth wide open but Joe did not realise that.

This 1952 by-election was as I have mentioned caused by the death of P.J. Ruttledge. Ruttledge had been in de Valera's first cabinet and to me at any rate, was one of the nicest, less controversial members of that cabinet. He was good company, was a great raconteur and had a considerable fondness for whiskey.

Paddy Ruttledge was a native of Raheen, outside Ballina and originally belonged to a firm of solicitors in Dublin, Ruttledge and McKenna. They were both TD's and when the split came over the Treaty, McKenna was reputed to have said: 'Well, I can't go back to Mullagh in Co. Cavan and say I'm going anti-Treaty. It would be more than my life is worth.' So they decided that one would go one way and the other another, and the practice split up. That particular McKenna incidentally, was an uncle of the great actor T.P. McKenna.

Ruttledge resigned from the cabinet because of ill health in 1941 but his ill health did not prevent him from representing Mayo – though resident in Dublin – and attending the constituency no more than twice a year while at the same time becoming Solicitor General to the Wards of Court. I remember at the time an article in the *People's Press* then edited and, I think, owned, by a character called Jimmy Shan McLoughlin from Buncrana. I always remember the last paragraph of his editorial. He said – and I believe I am quoting him accurately – that after all, perhaps Mr Ruttledge was to be commended for accepting this lucrative post. It would pay him much more than a ministerial salary, he having wisely decided that it was more profitable to look after the interests of the official lunatics of this country and the £1,700 a year that went with it, than to represent the interests of the unofficial lunatics of North Mayo who voted for him.

That was typical of the hard-hitting style of the time, especially in the provincial newspapers. The current sensitivity to the laws of libel would make that sort of journalism a very dangerous and hazardous occupation today.

I think in fact, that Ruttledge was glad to get out of the cabinet because he wanted an even tougher line against the IRA than was being pursued by the de Valera Government in the 1940s.

The Fianna Fáil candidate in that election was Phelim Calleary, father of the present Mayo TD, Sean Calleary. Phelim Calleary had been a life long friend of Ruttledge, and his already strong position was strengthened by the fact that he held the position of senior engineer with the County Council and thus had some influence over the granting or non-granting of housing and indeed the filling of County Council jobs. There was also a Clann na Talmhan candidate Frank Devaney from Lahardaun and a very decent man he was. The Clann na Poblachta candidate was Martin McGrath from Ballina.

I have to say in fairness to Joe Leneghan that he worked harder than anybody else in that particular campaign in which, by the way, I got the biggest Fine Gael vote ever, in the Barony of Erris, and in Ballycroy and Achill. That was partly because my roots are in that area, and partly because of the work of Joe Leneghan. The same couldn't be said of the Crossmolina and Ballina areas where the sitting TD for Fine Gael was resident, and of course, as is notorious in by-elections, sitting TD's rarely give full support to a by-election candidate, knowing full well that a good by-election run almost invariably guarantees election in the subsequent general election. Consequently, the effort in that area was not what it should have been with the result that we lost, though not for that reason alone.

So Phelim Calleary won that election – he and I were to be political opponents for much of my political life. On the surface a somewhat dour man, in private he was an extremely pleasant and straight man. When he was Ruttledge's right-hand man he had refused to take the oath necessary to become the county council engineer. In this he contrasted with another local pillar of Fianna Fáil and later a Senator,

T.P. Flanagan who, also incidentally, was a major figure in the Knights of Columbanus. Flanagan had no difficulty with the oath and later became County Engineer for Mayo. He was totally partisan. For example, he did not like the Healys, who ran a fine hotel in Pontoon, because they did not subscribe to his views. He brought the tarmacadam to within a mile of the hotel and then stopped. Later, on the Bellacorick/Castlebar road he brought the tarmacadam to a point at Beltra Lake where he used to cast his line. But his chief claim to fame was building a bridge at Ballylahan *over* which the water flowed. It became a tourist attraction. People came from all over Mayo every Sunday to see the water flowing over the bridge.

Not surprisingly I made great capital out of this, and it featured in many of my speeches, much to Flanagan's annoyance. Many years later, on his election to the Senate, he accused me of skullduggery with the Coalition government over the purchase of eight acres of land in Mayo from the Land Commission at a ridiculously low price. As it happened I had bought the land when Thomas Derrig of Fianna Fáil was Minister for Lands and there had been no irregularity of any sort. Of course there was no apology, but then I didn't think there would be.

After the 1952 by-election I went back to my law practice knowing that I would be a candidate in the next election which came sooner than expected in 1954. The election was precipitated by the result of two successful by-elections for Fine Gael, Stephen Barrett was elected in Cork and George Coburn in Louth. Sean Lemass was absent in London, and de Valera made a statement which considerably irritated Lemass – he told me so himself later – when he (de Valera) said: 'Of course, the people will now have to be consulted,' when in Lemass's view there was really no need to.

The election took place in the mid-summer of 1954 and after my by-election performance I was automatically a candidate. For the first time I made an impact on Ballina where my strong supporters included Dr Aubrey Burke, father of our President. Among my opponents were Denis Gallagher, later a Fianna Fáil Minister, but then running for Clann na Poblachta.

As it turned out I was five votes ahead of Pat Browne, our outgoing TD, on the first count and stayed ahead of him on all subsequent counts, helped by the fact that two of the other candidates, James Ginnelly of Achill (an aspirant Hyde Park corner orator), and Martin McGrath of Ballina, who ran for Clann na Poblachta transferred heavily to me. My victory was somewhat lessened by the fact that I was replacing Patrick Browne who had given 17 years service to Fine Gael and to his county.

I remember being carried shoulder high through the streets of Ballina which I have to say is a physically uncomfortable experience and it reminded me of other occasions when I had lost, particularly later in 1961 when in the loneliness of defeat nobody was around in the Imperial Hotel except my good friend Tony Chambers and it bore in on me the truth of an old adage: 'Success has a thousand fathers, failure is an orphan'.

So at the age of 40, on my sixth attempt, I had been elected to Dáil Eireann. I was no stranger to Leinster House but when I visit the place these days and look at the type of facilities available to TD's and Senators, I look back without nostalgia to the type of facilities which were available to us. Our salary was £624 per annum. We paid for our own post. Local phone calls were free (a lot of use to a TD from North Mayo!). There were no secretaries, and if you wanted one you paid out of your own salary. We did have a travel allowance which helped to keep the car on the road – but not much more and did not cover travel within a constituency.

The Fine Gael leadership was somewhat anomolous. Dick Mulcahy was the leader of Fine Gael, even though John A. Costello had been Taoiseach from 1948 - 1951 and was about to be re-elected Taoiseach. Costello would certainly have been seen in the country as the 'real' leader.

I discovered early on that the relationship between them was uncomfortable. Mulcahy, as a former Chief of Staff, with the rigidity and austerity of his army training was not well placed to obtain or inspire the best in a voluntary organisation. Costello on the other hand, was warm and generous, ever ready to help in any situation, either in law or in politics.

Another of the Civil War generation, and one I knew before I became a TD, was Sean McEoin. Although an army man, unlike Mulcahy, he had no trace of army austerity. He was a pleasant country man with tremendous natural ability, mostly unchannelled. I was later to travel all of Ireland with him in the 1959 Presidential campaign and we shared many conversations. I could see then, that his kindness, to which tributes were paid by British Army Officers when he was on trial for his life, was manifest in his every utterance. He never spoke unkindly of anybody.

I remember later in 1959 when the front bench of Fine Gael was considering a Presidential candidate; finally when the near-consensus appeared to be in favour of not contesting the election at all, it came to Sean McEoin's turn to speak. He said that while he did not wish to contest the election, that if he did not do so, he would be betraying his old friend and colleague, Michael Collins. Suddenly the whole scene changed.

The most dynamic senior figure in Fine Gael was Gerard Sweetman, and in 1954 he was appointed as Minister for Finance in Costello's second Inter-Party Government. He was not the kind of person one would expect to be as popular among rural people as he in fact was. Sweetman and myself had a sort of love/hate relationship which was based on great mutual respect. He was a worker who would not ask anybody to do something he would not do himself. He was a man of great courage and had an integrity that was often mistaken for ruthlessness. His sudden death in 1963 was a great national loss and a personal loss to me. I still retain a relationship with his family.

Coming into his second term as Minister for Agriculture and now back in the Fine Gael Party was James Dillon, by any standards a remarkable man. His father, John Dillon, had featured in many of our fireside discussions in my youth, and my father was always a great admirer and a staunch defender of John Dillon, right until the day he died. Like my father, I always believed that he never got sufficient credit for his pleas in the House of Commons to have the lives of the 1916 leaders spared, and I believed also, that many of the great contributions of the Parliamentary Party have been very unfairly treated by history.

Liam Cosgrave was no stranger to me when I entered Leinster House. I had known him since his schoolboy days and he used to holiday in Carna in Josie Mongan's hotel. Loyalty, then as now was his greatest quality. Law-abiding, respect for democracy and an eternal anxiety to do the right thing at the right time (as he showed in 1968 when he was prepared to resign as Party Leader on the P.R. issue, and again in late 1972 when he defied his party on the night of the Dublin bombs) were also among his great characteristics. But more of this anon.

I settled in very quickly to the life of a back bench TD. Of course, being a back bencher when your party is in Government does restrict your freedom of manoeuvre and reduces the number of targets available to you.

One of my first contributions was on 9 February 1955, concerning the question of tourism. I argued that after agriculture, tourism had the greatest potential for development and was one of our great natural resources. I stressed that unless our secondary roads were of good quality the tourist would not have access and would not be tempted to visit our great beauty spots. I was critical of the '*Tóstal*', then in full swing, arguing that it took much more than bunting and balls of light and what Dublin wits called 'the tomb of the unknown gurrier' on O'Connell Bridge to build a substantial tourist industry. I was particularly critical of the numerous derelict sites around the country and I believe I was the first person to advocate a 'tidy towns' competition.

I also contributed on issues such as the Land Commission, fisheries and rural development. My principal interest was education and my contributions there were as often in Irish as in English. I was particularly critical of the teaching of Irish in our schools and felt that we had wasted the past 30 years. I felt very strongly that Fianna Fáil had politicised the language issue, and made people cynical about it. I felt as passionately then as I do now that, as I said in 1955: 'The Irish language is our language, the language of our people, and as such it is right and proper that it should be given national rather than political treatment!' I also felt at the time – and indeed the recent Culliton Report echoes what I said then – that our educational system was too academic and that we should put far more resources into upgrading our vocational sector.

One particular target of mine was the preparatory colleges for those who would go on for training as national teachers. I felt the students all came from the same backgrounds – generally rural and Roman Catholic – that they did not have the chance to mix with people from other backgrounds and as a result were narrow in their views and had not had their curiosity excited – something I felt was at the very heart of good teaching. I urged the abolition of these preparatory colleges.

Looking back on the debates, I am amused that for somebody as technologically illiterate as I am, I was in one respect at least, ahead of my time. I wanted the updating of education by the installation of a 'wire-recording system', so that the student could fully appreciate the defects in his speech, and thence set about repairing these defects. I also wanted 'wire-recording systems' as they were then called, used in language teaching.

I urged also that we had a responsibility to take a much harder look at, and devote greater resources to, the problems of the mentally handicapped.

It was in June 1955 that I first spoke on a Gaeltacht motion and during the course of that debate I outlined my philosophy on the Gaeltacht, which I saw largely in terms of development. It was my view that so long as these areas were subject to emigration: 'You might as well be throwing money down the drain as spending it in an effort to keep Irish as the spoken language of the people in those areas. It is only when the people are in a position to survive, grow up, finish their schooling, engage in local activities of a commercial nature that will provide a living for them, and afterwards marry and settle down in those areas and bring up families as their fathers did before them, that we will get the continuity of language that is so necessary in order to preserve it.'

I was by and large a well-behaved and constructive back bencher and was only thrown out on one occasion. This arose out of a row between my Mayo colleague, Michael Moran and myself. I accused him of telling lies. I believe I was right. In any event I refused to withdraw the charge and I was ordered out of the House. But that was an exception.

In late 1955 John A. Costello was clearly worried about the way in which the Government was operating and by a lack of energy in some areas. He called me aside one night after a party meeting and he said to me that he would be bringing in a new Ministers and Secretaries Act, with a view to setting up a new department of the Gaeltacht. He told me that when that was done he proposed to appoint me as a Parliamentary Secretary to both the Gaeltacht and Education with a view, as he said, to letting General Mulcahy take the Gaeltacht, in which he had an interest and that Education would be under me. He flattered me by telling me that he felt that I had energy and new ideas to bring to that department.

I strongly supported the decision to set up a separate department of the Gaeltacht. I believed that it wasn't possible to improve the position of Irish unless there was an economically viable community in the

Gaeltacht areas and, that in particular, the difficulty of bringing in industry to the Gaeltacht was hampered by the fact that it was in the hands of people who necessarily might not know Irish and certainly would not know the areas in question. Specifically however, I emphasised the need for economic development and wanted the new Department to be called the 'Department for the Development of the Gaeltacht'.

In any event on 2 June 1956 I was appointed Parliamentary Secretary to the Departments of the Gaeltacht and Education. I took up my duties in Marlborough Street by first of all being introduced by General Mulcahy to the 'top brass' and in the line waiting to greet me was an inspector of the vocational education branch who had recommended my dismissal a few years before when I was working for Comhairle Le Leas Oige. The reason why he recommended my dismissal need not detain us here. It was more of a misunderstanding than anything else and in the event I was simply moved to Mount Street, not dismissed. However as I came towards him in the line I saw him blushing. I smiled and simply said: 'Mr X, Man proposes; God disposes.' We shook hands and that was that.

After that ceremony was over the late Larry Murray, then Secretary of the Department of Education, put me into the room of a senior official, Terry Raftery, because he was on holidays. No room had been set aside for me, and I was soon to experience how civil servants neutralise their political 'Masters'.

I was given a file of some considerable size to read. This purported to be some form of initiation into the great educational mysteries of Marlborough Street. In fact it concerned the setting up, or non-setting up, of what was then known as a 'secondary top' in the national school in Strokestown, Co. Roscommon. I have read a lot in my time, but never have I come across such prevarication, postponement, adjournments, further considerations, active considerations, all amounting to utter bilge and the ultimate non-creation of a 'top'.

What followed was even more illuminating. Having finished this irrelevant file and not being prepared to sit around looking out a window in Marlborough Street, as I never found the drainpipes particularly attractive, I took up the file, walked across the corridor and knocked on the door of Mr Larry Murray's office. He got up in a rather excited state and said: 'Mr Minister why did you not ring for an usher?'
'Why?'
'To carry the file.'
I later discovered that at that time in the Civil Service nobody over the range of executive office carried a file from room to room. An usher was always sent for.

It was not a very promising start. Then I was transferred to a dark room in the Department of Education in Hume Street. My personal secretary, Seamus Breathnach, and my typist, a very charming girl, Miss Betty Hunt from Kilkelly, Co. Mayo came with me. That was all.

Nobody came near us. Nobody told us what to do and we were left to our own devices. It was as if the Civil Service had decided to freeze me out. We remained in that room until October and I think that people in the building must have thought we were photographers because of the darkness of the room in which we were incarcerated.

It was all very odd but in some ways the attitude of the Department of Education was best summed up in the personality of its Secretary, Mr Murray. He was a gentleman, very mild of manner but like so many of the other heads of departments in those days he was content to let things slide. You can do no wrong, you can make no mistakes, if you do nothing. That seemed to be the prevailing philosophy of the day.

In October, when the new Department formally came into existence, I was appointed as Minister for the Gaeltacht and I moved to new offices in Earlsfort Terrace. They weren't very lavish, not that they had to be because the staff was small, but for the most part they were good.

My main disappointment was that I didn't have the opportunity of appointing the Secretary to the Department. That was done by General Mulcahy because of his power as Minister and of course it was done with the approval of the Minister for Finance.

Rightly or wrongly I did not trust the person who had been appointed. He had begun his civil service career as personal secretary to Dr Ryan, the Fianna Fáil Minister and a brother-in-law of General Mulcahy. At this point I don't know whether I was right or wrong to ignore him. I may have been unfair and certainly he must have complained in that regard because James Dillon said to me one day when I was sitting beside him at a cabinet meeting: 'Pat, I consult with my Secretary about three or four times a day – I'm told that you don't consult with your Secretary at all.' 'No, I don't, because you could hardly have an awful lot of respect for the Permanent Head of a Department who spends his time in the bay window looking out to see who is late or who is early coming in, and coming downstairs and instructing the porter to draw the red line under those who are late.'

One of the first things I did was to abolish the compulsory signing of the attendance book. I introduced what today would be called 'flexi-time'. All I asked was that I got an honest day's work and I had no time for petty rules and restrictions. The staff responded well and we had a good relationship.

Incidentally, on the day of my appointment, 24 October 1956, I was representing the Government, of which I was not yet a member at the funeral of the late James Fitzgerald Kenny at Carnacon outside Castlebar. When I came back to the Dáil I discovered there was great excitement. Fianna Fáil had decided to oppose my appointment. In the event the vote was won by the Government by 67 votes to 62.

The Fianna Fáil opposition, led by Eamon de Valera, centred on the extravagence of a new Department at this time; my lack of administrative experience was called into question by Sean MacEntee, while Neal Blaney attacked a speech I had made in the Dáil in which I said that there was no future for Irish as a spoken language unless bi-lingualism was going to flourish. Blaney said this attitude made me unacceptable to the people of the Gaeltacht.

The Taoiseach vigorously defended me. I had come from the Mayo Gaeltacht, gone to a university in the Gaeltacht, had done my MA in the Irish language and was, in his words: 'An Irish scholar in the best sense.'

So, accompanied by the Taoiseach, General Mulcahy and some officials, we drove to Aras an Uachtaráin where Sean T. O'Kelly gave me my seal of office and a very hospitable welcome.

* * * *

My time in the Department of the Gaeltacht was short. There was very little I could do as I simply didn't have the resources. I never had a chance to introduce my own Estimate or to stamp my own personality on the Department.

I suppose my main achievement was the creation of what people, rather ironically, call the 'Lindsay Gaeltacht'. My fundamental reason for doing this was that I believe that the people of these particular areas, whether they were *fíor* Gaeltacht areas or not, had bad housing, bad sanitation and no water. I felt there was enough spoken Irish in these areas to give them the same chance of economic development as pertained in the *fíor* Gaeltacht and that as a result, the speaking and spread of Irish would be encouraged.

My other achievement was to appoint the late Sean Glynn as Assistant Secretary to the Department. I believe he made an impact and understood the Gaeltacht better than any of the resident civil servants.

I remember one day at a Cabinet meeting – if one can talk about Cabinet meetings with the recent, and very odd Supreme Court judgement on Cabinet confidentiality – James Dillon saying to me, as I was trying to get various pockets into the Gaeltacht: 'Pat, you're not suggesting they are native Irish speakers in Bangor Erris?' All I could say was: 'Well I'm not suggesting it, but I think that due to their economic circumstances, they would be entitled to whatever is going.' He said: 'Well that would not be my view.' I regret to say that it was James' view which prevailed.

* * * *

There were some bizarre situations in those days, especially on housing matters in the new Gaeltacht areas which pointed out to me, at any rate, the dead hand of officialdom.

One day after a Mass in Geesala, I met a great old friend of mine from the parish, Anthony Doherty. He said to me that although he had been voting for me all his life and had known me all of that time as well, he didn't know whether he should speak to me at all on that day. 'Why?'

'I've got a letter in my pocket from your Department, refusing me a housing grant.'

'Give me the letter.'

The reason given in the letter refusing the grant was that Irish was not the *gnáth theanga* of the household.

I put the letter in my pocket, came back to Dublin, called in the Housing Inspector and asked him what the *gnáth theanga* in that house was.

'Well, it wasn't Irish.'

'How do you know? With whom had you discussions in the house?'

'Oh' he said, 'Anthony Doherty himself.'

'Did he speak Irish?'

'He did.'

'And who else was in the house?'

'I didn't see anybody else.'

'Well, would it surprise you to know that Anthony Doherty lives alone and there is no *gnáth theanga,* unless you test him on what he said to the dog or the cat.'
The nett result was that I sanctioned the grant to Anthony Doherty.

However, the matter did not end there. Shortly afterwards, I had a visit at his request, from the Secretary of the Department carrying with him a copy of Street's *Local Government Law* and pointing out to me a paragraph saying that when the political head of a Department went against an inspector's report then the Secretary of the Department would be surcharged. I said to him: 'Would you care to read the paragraph before that?'

He did, and it was to the effect that when the political head of the Department made the decision there was no question of a surcharge. That was as much as he knew about Street's *Local Government Law.*

* * * *

During my time as Parliamentary Secretary, before I became Minister for the Gaeltacht, I did several tours to various districts with General Mulcahy. These districts were generally classified as Gaeltacht and Irish speaking districts and of course, as such, qualified for all the various grants which were then available.

One such visit was to Glencolmcille in Co. Donegal. I noticed on arrival that the entire village had been freshly painted and that the notices (which were all in Irish), were also freshly painted. There was a Guard of Honour for Mulcahy, and as he was taking the Guard of Honour I just stood back and watched what was going on. I think anybody who noticed me probably thought I was Mulcahy's driver. The children duly formed their Guard of Honour immediately beside the platform and they were all chanting 'Fáilte romhat a Aire'. However, as soon as the Guard of Honour broke up the girls immediately began to talk among themselves in sweet Donegal accents of the most pure English. The whole thing was all a charade. The only useful part of that day was meeting a priest who was interested in a few half ones. Exactly the same thing happened in Leenane in Connemara, where again, every showboard there had been changed to Irish for the purpose of persuading us of the Gaeltacht *bona fides* of the area.

* * * *

I enjoyed my short time in Cabinet, though it coincided with an economic and financial recession, resulting largely from the Suez crisis and the world depression. Even though there was very little we could do in the face of world circumstances, we were, as always happens to Governments, blamed. Unemployment and emigration were our major, indeed overiding pre-occupations in Cabinet. I remember one day leaving a Cabinet meeting, feeling thoroughly dejected and I remember, following me was Brendan Corish who put his hand on my shoulder and said: 'Cheer up, it's not always like that.' I said: 'Well I'm afraid it's going to be like that for my time anyway; because we're going out the next time.'

But I wasn't always so depressed, and I have to say that I had enormous respect for those with whom I served. We were a very united Government and that, I think, was due to the great influence exerted by three people in particular in that Cabinet. The first of course was the Taoiseach himself, John A. Costello. The second was the Attorney General, Paddy McGilligan, one of the great unsung architects of modern Ireland and one of the few genuine political philosophers the country has ever had. The third was the contribution made by Gerard Sweetman, as I said before, a man whose loss to this country is hard to estimate.

James Dillon was a strong influence too. I well remember when anything requiring a decision arose that if James wasn't happy that we had examined all aspects of the matter, he would preface his remarks by saying: 'I want to sound a Three Bell Warning' and when James sounded the 'Three Bell Warning', we all listened with respect and in the majority of cases, accepted his judgement. James, I believe had almost prophetic powers. Like Cassandra of old, he had an uncanny power to see into the future, but he also had the defect of Cassandra, that very few people believed him. He was a great man, a prodigious reader and of course, a splendid orator.

I had great time too for my colleagues from Clann na Talmhan. There was Joseph Blowick from Belcarra, outside Castlebar. He was a man of extraordinary ability which was untutored, untamed and often misdirected. Joe was a member of an extremely distinguished family, his brother having founded the Mission to China and several others of the family lay claim to significant achievements.

The person that I liked best in the cabinet was James Everett from Wicklow. He was a man of few words but of enormous intrinsic decency.

Michael Keyes was a Limerick man to whom Jim Kemmy recently paid a splendid and well-deserved tribute. Keyes was very quiet, and well respected; a man of great common sense. Brendan Corish was a gentleman to his fingertips. He and I had a long and affectionate relationship.

Bill Norton, I always thought was probably the best public speaker and certainly the best speaker in the Dáil and that included James Dillon and Jack Costello. Norton was incisive, sharp and devastating in debate. He had begun his life as a boy messenger in the post-office, had risen to run a powerful Trade Union and become Leader of the Labour Party, Tanaiste and Minister for Industry and Commerce. It took zeal and hard work to get where he did. He was a very fine man, a very fair man. I was very impressed by a remark of his one day in Cabinet, when there was some suggestion of letting off workers from Bord na Móna. He said: 'Look, the difference between their wages and what you get on the dole is about a pound or thirty shillings. Why cause an upheaval of this kind when it's not going to cost the country that much?' His view was accepted by the Cabinet.

Liam Cosgrave was Minister for External Affairs as it was then called. His contributions were always worthwhile. He had a great 'nose' for changing circumstances, a 'nose' and an instinct that would help him go in the right direction and make the right decisions. His clarity of thought was extraordinary. He was – indeed, happily, still is – a fair man and a very loyal man.

I never served in Government with Dr Noel Browne but I have to say that the character sketches of those who served with him in his book *Against the Tide* are, to my mind, grossly unfair. I have great admiration for Noel Browne and for what he did as the Minister for Health. I do not however, subscribe to the popular view that he alone succeeded in the eradication of tuberculosis from our country. Nothing could be further from the truth, because in fairness to the late Dr Jim Ryan, he had laid the foundation for this particular exercise in the 1947 Health Act, to which many useful contributions had been made by people like the late Dan Morrissey and several others from the Fine Gael front benches in the Dáil. When Noel Browne became the Minister for Health it is true that he applied himself with great vigour to the eradication of T.B., having both the medical and personal interest in it. But, it must be remembered, that he could not have achieved all that he did achieve, without the firm foundations of the 1947 Health Act, and for the fact that in Paddy McGilligan he had a caring Minister for Finance, who provided the money at a very difficult time. Indeed, Browne was lucky to find himself a member of a collectively caring Government – one of the best Governments this country has ever had.

It's a pity that in his book he took to task so many of his former colleagues on grounds that were unfair and irrelevant. For instance, in his description of the late Dr David Thornley, who was a friend of mine I am proud to say, his attribution of sexual ambivalence, is in my view, a disgraceful distortion, totally without foundation.

He had lots of other things to say about former colleagues. Can anything be more ridiculous than the charge that James Dillon had neither breadth of vision nor depth of thought? Noel Browne has said that James Dillon never said anything new and wasn't capable of original thought. Rubbish!

I dined several times with the late William Norton and I never saw any demonstration of the bad table manners attributed to him by Browne in his book. I think it destroys an otherwise good book to indulge in cheap shots of that kind, particularly at those who are no longer here to defend themselves. He refers to the late Dan Morrissey as 'mumbling and fumbling'. Nothing could be further from the truth. I had the privilege of knowing Dan Morrissey, his wife and all his family and I rarely came across a man of such deep feeling and common sense, particularly when he was dealing with the lot of ordinary people. It's a tribute to Dan Morrissey who was first elected to the Dáil as a member of the Labour Party, that when he subsequently stood in the 1932 election as an Independent in North Tipperary (he had been expelled from the Labour Party, along with Mr Richard Anthony of Cork, after he had voted with Mr Cosgrave's Government, on the Constitutional Amendment Act in the 1920s, for the protection of law and order) he topped the poll. In 1933 Morrissey joined Cumann na nGaedheal and as such, topped the poll once again. I prefer the people's judgement of such a man, to Noel Browne's spiteful and derogatory remarks. Not only did I know Dan Morrissey very well, but I also enjoyed the hospitality of his household, where I often stayed the night (having no lodgings of my own) in my leaner days. Indeed, Mrs Morrissey was one of the most kindly women I've come across – and I've come across many.

* * * *

We lost the election in 1957, Fine Gael lost ten seats. I held my own seat in North Mayo – one of the rare times I did so comfortably, but all in all it was a gloomy time.

When the new Dáil met, de Valera was elected Taoiseach for the last time. His Party had won 77 seats in the election and all we had to look forward to was a lengthy stay in opposition backed by a depressed and demoralised Party.

In some ways our situation is best summed up by an incident that happened after the defeat of Jack Costello as Taoiseach. We immediately headed back, as was the case in those days, to return our Seals of Office (or as I called them, our Sodality Medals) to the President, Sean T. O'Kelly at Áras an Uachtarain. I have to say his manner towards us was quite different to what it had been the previous time. On that occasion he gave us a drink; this time he did not. It was a bleak day.

But in any event we drove down the Quays on McBirney's side, '40 paces from O'Connell Bridge' as the old ad used to say. I was sitting in the back of the ministerial Dodge, right behind the driver, the late Sergeant Paddy Byrne. Sitting beside him was the Secretary of the Government, Maurice Moynihan. In the back of the car, also in the middle was Jack Costello with his head down and looking totally unlike the kind of man he was – he looked gruff whereas he was the kindest of men. On his left was James Dillon and as we passed the old Irish House, which is a public house with figurines outside it – it's gone now as a result of the Wood Quay fiasco – James Dillon said: 'You know, I never fail to be intrigued by that old Irish House.'

'If you saw it four times a day coming from the Four Courts,' said Costello, 'you wouldn't be a bit impressed.'

The conversation continued with James Dillon saying: 'You know I was never in a public house in my life except my own in Ballaghaderreen, which I sold because when I saw people going home having spent so much money on drink, I decided that they were depriving their families of the essentials.' Then, to my consternation, Jack Costello said that he was in a public house only once in his life, in Terenure, and was nearly choked by a bottle of orange. I was totally appalled by this state of affairs and I expressed my feelings as follows: ' *****, I now know why we are going in this direction today and why we are out of touch with the people.'

For we were out of touch. The public house is the countryman's club, where everything is discussed and where contacts are made. And here was a Prime Minister of an agricultural country, in a public house only once in his life and the Minister for Agriculture who was responsible for brewing and distilling had never been in a public house except for his own. How could we be going in any other direction?

* * * *

The year 1959 was a year of change in Irish politics. De Valera stood for the Presidency and Sean Lemass took over as leader of Fianna Fáil. I had got to know Sean Lemass quite well on our trips to Inter-Parliamentary Union meetings and had come to form a very high opinion of him. He was direct, unpretentious and open. His energy and his enthusiasm were very evident. My only complaint would be that he had little or no understanding of rural Ireland. He was the essential city man.

In Fine Gael too it was a year of change. General Mulcahy decided to stand down as party leader – though in reality most people regarded Jack Costello as the real leader. It was an unsatisfactory arrangement and it was James Dillon who brought matters to a head with his customary bluntness. He said the party needed a full-time leader, and as far as he was concerned that narrowed the field down to two people – Liam Cosgrave and himself.

Jack Costello toyed with the idea of running but was dissuaded especially since he was not prepared to be a full-time leader. So it was a contest between James and Liam. Although I was personally closer to Liam, I supported James.

On the day of the election I was sitting beside Liam Cosgrave and I wrote down: 'James 57 plus 10, 67, Liam - 39 plus 30, 69'. I said: 'Do you ever think you could possibly last as leader for 30 years – you're too young, your time has not yet come – I'm voting for James.' So he said: 'Fair enough – thank you for telling me.'

James was elected leader and he was a great leader in many ways. He was a leader that inspired people from one public meeting to another, but I don't think that the inspiration was sustained during the intervals. Fianna Fáil always used a very successful piece of propaganda against him, that he always regretted the fact that he wasn't in the House of Commons instead of being in the Dáil – all of which was utter bunkum because James Dillon was as patriotic a man as any I have met during the whole course of my political career or since.

* * * *

The years between 1957-1961 were fairly uneventful. I devoted much more of my time to law, but I did not neglect my constituency business. I was not a believer in the clinic and never have been. I wanted things done through the party organisation or through community committees where we could benefit the community by way of drainage, forestry, fisheries, better roads and other facilities. I was never interested in the fellow who pulled you to one side and secretly asked you for something. My automatic reaction was that he was seeking something to which he was not entitled, or something to which somebody else was entitled and he wasn't.

I did not neglect my constituency. My style may have been unusual but I did visit it three weekends each month and went to different parts of it. It was a wild and far-flung constituency, geographically a difficult constituency, as is any constituency where there are large inlets and bays. Donegal would be a similar example, Galway to a certain extent is the same, as are West Cork and Kerry. From my own geographical location I was standing with my back to the sea where there were no votes and had to fight my way inland. It is understandable as to why it took me so long ultimately to get a grip on the Fine Gael vote in Ballina town and Crossmolina and Killala – although I have to say Killala supported me from the very beginning as did Newport. In fact, in the 1937 election I actually headed the poll in Newport.

In any event I did not do well in the election of 1961 and lost my seat. In that election, Joe Leneghan ran as an Independent and since he came from the same part of the county as I did, that cut into my vote. In turn, that allowed Miko Browne, running for the first time, to get ahead of me and win the one Fine Gael seat. Our percentage of the vote remained constant but Miko pipped me for the one seat. Joe Leneghan was elected at the expense of Fianna Fáil and, like the good Fine Gael man he had been, he immediately supported the Fianna Fáil Government of Sean Lemass. Along with Frank Sherwin he supported that Government through thick and thin from 1961 to 1965 and eventually ran for Fianna Fáil in the 1965 General Election where he was my principal opponent, but more of that later.

Having lost my seat in 1961, I was tempted to leave politics altogether. My law practice was improving, my family were young and the difficulties of representing a far-flung distant constituency were considerable. However, after my defeat and as I have said before, defeat can be a very lonely time, James Dillon showed me considerable kindness and asked me, even though I was no longer a TD, to attend the first post-election meeting of the Fine Gael front bench. It was a kindness which I will always remember even though I did feel somewhat out of place amongst all of my other colleagues who had been successfully returned even though Fine Gael had not won the election, and even though we were facing another long period in opposition.

James insisted that I run for the Senate. I was nominated on the Industrial and Commercial Panel and for the first time in my life I was elected with a quota. I had a fraction of a vote over the quota and in fact when the new Senate met I was elected as Leas Cathaoirleach or Deputy Speaker.

The change to the Senate was somewhat dramatic. It is a much more low-key type of chamber and there is little of the cut and thrust of the Dáil about it. Being Deputy Speaker meant I did not have the luxury of walking out during some of the very bad debates which took place from time to time. I was obliged to stay to the bitter end, but I was always grateful for the ornate beauty of the Senate ceiling, one of the great architectural gems of Leinster House, and there can hardly have been a square inch of that ceiling that I did not study during some of the insufferably long contributions.

However, there were some outstanding members of the Senate. I remember in particular the contributions of some of the Trinity Senators. Senator Stanford, a leonine, handsome man was probably the finest of all the contributors. John Ross, father of Senator Shane Ross, also made distinctive and distinguished contributions as indeed did most, but not all, of the university Senators of that time. Their contributions however were generally academic and rarely bore little relation to the normal everyday needs of the people. That lack was made up by some of the party Senators: strong, generally silent men, who made very solid contributions from time to time. I remember Senator Joseph Mary Mooney from Drumshanbo with whom I had violent disagreements about the merits of *An Tóstal*. He was a very decent man, very localised – everything centered around Leitrim, particularly Drumshanbo. I remember one day in the Chair, after I was a bit tired of hearing of Drumshanbo. I said to him half-joking, half-in-earnest: 'By the way Senator Mooney, if you mention Drumshanbo, I will rule you out of order.' He laughed and continued and he made a good contribution and his last word was 'Drumshanbo'. He sat down and smiled. What could I do except smile in reply?

Another man who was a serious contributor and a very good debater was Senator Con Desmond, father of Barry Desmond of the Labour Party. He was a thoughtful, well-organised, serious man whose contributions were always worth listening to and always smacked of sound common sense. Among the others there was Eoin Ryan, again a serious contributor, not too frequent, but whenever he did speak his business acumen shone through, and enlightened his contributions.

The Leader of the House for Fianna Fáil in those days was a great character called Tommy Mullins. He had been a TD way back in the 1920s and had some disagreement at that time with de Valera and lost the party whip – indeed he left the House for quite some time. He eventually came back as General Secretary of Fianna Fáil and was nominated as one of the Taoiseach's cricket team – the 11 – in 1961 and became Leader of the House. He and I got on very well together. He was a great story teller and a man of no malice.

I remember on the occasion of the death of Pope John XXIII Senator Mullins was called upon to propose the vote of sympathy. He made a speech, a comprehensive and colourful speech and then we all stood for our two minutes silence. After we sat down he came over to ask me how he had done. 'You did great – sure you had him in everything except the old IRA – and you came close to that.' His reply, while perfectly friendly, is not repeatable.

In some ways it was a happy, indeed happy-go-lucky House. There were some who were unco-operative and unfriendly but that's true of any gathering. One man who greatly enlivened the House at the time was Gerry l'Estrange. Gerry was a powerful interrupter and showed no fear or awe in the face of even the most formidable Government contributors. He came to me one day and said: 'James wants me to speak on the Army Pensions Bill. What will I say?'

'Well, I think a very good opening line would be to say that it is your opinion that the GPO was more crowded in 1916 than was the Mayflower.' Gerry got up and started his speech with this line, where upon the entire Fianna Fáil benches nearly came across in an earthquake on top of him. He looked at me. I looked at the Duke of Leinster's ceiling, paying no attention to him at all, but what really did surprise me was not that Gerry L'Estrange said what I had told him to say, or thought that it might not cause some trouble, but it was the fact that the Fianna Fáil people really understood the reference to the Mayflower, and reacted accordingly.

The Senate however was not a particularly serious body. In spite of the high quality of some of the speeches and the seriousness of some – though not all, by a long shot – of the Senators, it really made no impact. This was mainly because the Government did not allow it do its work. Governments rarely, if ever, accepted Senate amendments so that the whole exercise became a bit pointless. I have always felt that there is a place for the Senate but only if Governments take it seriously and undertake genuine and proper reform.

* * * *

This is probably as good a time as any to reflect on some of the characters of Leinster House in my day.

I remember one evening in the old restaurant of Leinster House, I was sitting at a table with the late Alfie Byrne, many times Lord Mayor of Dublin and Oliver J. Flanagan, that greatest of survivors. They were discussing how a TD should behave whenever a bereavement occurred in his constituency. Alfie told Oliver that when he saw a death, particularly of a man in his constituency, if he could not get to the funeral, he should write immediately to the widow, bemoaning her great loss and saying at the same time that his own loss was very great too as the deceased had been his great personal friend. In my naivety I butted in and said: 'Suppose he was not this great personal friend' and Alfie looked at me as the green-horn I was and said: 'My dear fellow, he is not in a position to deny it!' Oliver took that message to heart and used it throughout his entire parliamentary life.

Tom Kyne was an extremely interesting man, bright and possessed of a quick wit. One time I asked him what kind of a Labour organisation he had in Waterford. His reply was that he had no such thing as an organisation; he relied on hatchet-men. I was quite sympathetic to that view as I had started my own political career in North Mayo with hatchet-men and retained them throughout. Kyne however told me that a hatchet-man had three disadvantages: one was that he might die; the second was that he might embezzle money and the third was that he might cause serious embarrassment by making the daughter of somebody important in the party pregnant.

I could never understand during the Inter-Party Government why Tom Kyne was not made a Parliamentary Secretary. In my view he should have been, but for some reason he probably was not *persona grata* with those in his own party or somebody else in the parties comprising the government. He would have been a strong addition.

Dan Breen I never met. He always intrigued me. Here was a man who was in parliament for a considerable time and had never learned anything of parliamentary practice and procedure. It would have been very simple to stand up and say 'on a point of order', or 'a Ceann Comhairle', but he never did any of these things. He would stand up, crack his thumb and forefinger and shout at the Ceann Comhairle saying, 'Hello there'.

Mick Donnellan was the founder of the Clann na Talmhan Party. I have a little suspicion that he was somehow connected with the Fianna Fáil party before that and the initiation of Clann na Talmhan may well have been an effort to establish a political niche for himself.

If that is so he was very successful. He wasn't a great orator; his voice was raucous, but he was a great constituency worker. I was with him one day at a Fair Day meeting in Ballygar, in the General Election of 1957. For some reason there happened to be present a reporter from the *Manchester Guardian*. He didn't speak too highly of me because I had abused some interrupter, which I had, but I thought his description of Donnellan's voice was tremendous. The *Manchester Guardian* reporter described Donnellan as 'speaking with a voice like a tractor in low gear'.

Of all the people who came into the Dáil before my time, one of the more impressive was Pa O'Donnell of Burtonport in Donegal. He was the Inter-Party choice for a by-election in West Donegal in 1949. I was up there on several week-ends speaking on his behalf. He had a great sense of local touch. For instance, one evening I heard him begin a meeting, not by saying 'ladies and gentlemen', or 'friends', or anything else. He began dramatically 'People of the lower Rosses'.

Incidentally, while chosen as the Inter-Party candidate, he belonged to the Fine Gael persuasion but would not allow himself be described as the Fine Gael candidate. He called himself an Inter-Party candidate and he won the by-election against a strong Fianna Fáil candidate, the late Joe Brennan, who subsequently came into the Dáil.

Pa O'Donnell was a solicitor with a wide-ranging practice over virtually the whole of Donegal and even into Sligo. Among his many clients were well-known poachers of fish. Generally they were convicted in the District Court, whereupon Pa immediately appealed and arranged things in such a way that all appeals would be heard in Letterkenny by the Circuit Court judge. Pa would go there; so would all the bailiffs, but none of the actual appellants. When the cases were called, Pa would solemnly rise and withdraw the appeal against conviction and throw himself on the mercy of the court on behalf of the appellants. Now the reason for this, as I heard afterwards and I have no reason to disbelieve it, was that while all the bailiffs were assembled in Letterkenny, the defending appellants were poaching the rivers and the sea in order to collect enough fish to sell so that, among other things, they could give their solicitor a decent fee.

Cormac Breslin, the deputy Speaker of Dáil Eireann in my time came from the picturesque village of Bunbeg in North-West Donegal. He was a man of gentle humour but nonetheless, firm in seeing that parliamentary procedure was correctly observed. He was kind to newcomers who would be likely to make mistakes. I got to know him extremely well on a trip to Japan with John Moher on an I.P.U. Conference. It was there that I really got to know these two men. The shrewdness of Breslin was in direct contrast with the naivety of John Moher.

Jim Hession of Tuam had been elected in 1951. He had, like Henry Kenny in South Mayo in 1954, got back the Fine Gael seat in that North Galway constituency. He and Michael Donnellan got on extremely well together and I would say that it was the pooling and transfer of votes that really elected Hession in 1951. In any event he was re-elected in 1954 and he was in the Dáil with me until 1957. During that time he rarely if ever spoke. He certainly never asked a question. Once, on the programme *Looking West* with Jim Fahy, I was asked if I could explain Hession's failure as a politician and my reply was, that Hession was not a failure. He was totally uninterested in political success. By any standards Hession was a solicitor and a very good solicitor at that. In fact, in my experience with the Western Circuit, he was easily the best.

During my time in Dáil Eireann, perhaps one of the most colourful and gentlemanly characters was Maurice Dockrell. He had a keen interest in classical music and would talk about it avidly, not in any kind of superior manner, but he obviously thought everybody would share the same interest and the same enthusiasm as himself. I can recall him talking about the music libraries in the great hotels of Europe. That wasn't the kind of conversation one would generally get at a bar and Maurice was pretty frequently in the bar in Leinster House. He was a generous man and from time to time if we met on social outings he would always invite us back to his home. He poured drinks copiously and one felt one was there for hours to come with plenty of drink flowing. Having given everybody a drink however – and they were large drinks – he would take his place at the piano, play and forget all about everybody else. We generally left without even saying good-bye to him and he didn't even notice our departure.

Another Mayo man who did well in North County Dublin was the late Paddy Burke. Paddy was a nice man and a genuinely decent man but he had a fatal tendency to indulge in sanctimonious nonsense. It was well known that he went to every funeral in North County Dublin, and equally well known, that when the priest had finished his duties by the graveside, Paddy would step in and say: 'We will now finish with a decade of the rosary for the dear man gone.' He was quite disappointed in 1957 when, having brought Kevin Boland in on his coat-tails, he himself was ignored for either a senior or a junior ministry and Boland instead was given a full ministry. I have to confess I have a great liking for his son Ray.

Brendan Corish was a Labour deputy with a difference. He had a good sense of values and was very solid in advice, when he chose to give it, on any subject. I recall Brian Quinn interviewing me after my retirement and asking me if I had any difficulties in government with the Labour members of that cabinet. I said I wasn't very long there – but he asked me anyway about whether there were differences of ideology. 'Ideological differences,' I said, 'the four Labour members, Corish, Keyes, Everett and Norton were to the right of Gerry Sweetman.

Michael Pat Murphy, the Labour Deputy for what was then West Cork was a jovial man with a curious mixture of the serious. I got to know him well and found him a most interesting companion. I well recall, on an I.U.P. trip, him asking an Indian MP in Vienna what his majority was. The Indian said: 'Somewhere in the neighbourhood of 300,000.'

'By God', said Michael Pat, 'that's what you'd call a safe seat.' Then he asked the Indian what he did when parliament wasn't sitting in New Delhi and the Indian's reply was: 'Well, I look after the social welfare interests of my constituents: roads, drains, water supplies and such things.'

'By God,' said Michael Pat, 'you could represent West Cork.'

Another great character, towards the end of my time, was Paddy Donegan – gentle, jovial, generous but linguistically accident prone.

* * * *

Shortly after my being elected, I received a letter from a man well known to me saying he had been dismissed from his position as Principal of a primary school because it was alleged by the parish priest that he had been interfering with senior girls. The letter continued without elaboration or exoneration: 'Be that as it may, I need a reference for a school elsewhere and I was hoping that you would give me such a reference.' At first I was doubtful but having made enquiries, I became satisfied that this particular parish priest had made an error and, as parish priests sometimes can make errors, can even be reckless and sometimes unjust, I gave the reference and I am glad to say that he finished his teaching career without further interruption.

Another letter I received is an example of the Irish attachment to the land. A couple, quite near Newport in Co. Mayo, had married rather late in life and had one child, a girl. As a girl they were afraid she would not inherit the land and so, in accordance with practice, they brought her suitably robed to the parish church and had her baptised as a boy. She was, however, also given a girl's name and grew up as a girl in the locality without anybody ever knowing of the baptismal certificate or paying any great heed to it. Problems arose, however, when she applied for a pension and had to produce her baptismal certificate. At this stage I was called in and I was asked if I could do anything about it. I was reading the letter and chuckling a bit to myself in the corridor of Leinster House when I met Hetty Behan, one of the great women in Fianna Fáil, and I showed her the letter. She said: 'Well, I thought I had read everything, but obviously I hadn't. Come on down to Sean MacEntee, the Minister, and we will see what we can do about it.' We went down, MacEntee graciously saw us and read the letter and said it required investigation. I thought to myself that I would not like to be part of that sort of investigation, but MacEntee to his credit followed it up and, on receipt of suitable affidavits, granted her her old age pension.

* * * *

Talking of MacEntee reminds me of a night in the course of the General Election of 1948 when we were all assembled at a pub in Achill Sound. When I say 'all', I mean people of all parties and, in the course of the conversation, several political personalities were mentioned and a man called Eddie Corrigan who had been interned during the war – I could never understand why because he hadn't even a shot-gun – asked me if I had ever met Maginty'.
I said: 'I don't know anybody called Maginty.'
'Ah you know the fellow who insulted John Dillon's son.'
I said: 'You probably mean MacEntee?'
'Not at all' he said, 'Sure he is the same as the Magintys of Dooriel'.
'I see,' said I, 'I have never met him, except fleetingly, but I can tell you what I am told, namely that socially he is a very gentle, calm man and good company, but that when he is interrupted, whether in the Dáil or on a public platform, he goes berserk and loses his temper.'

'Well,' said Eddie, 'that's understandable.' I enquired why he saw it as understandable. He said, very simply: 'It was a clash between nature and learning, and nature always wins.'

One of the most pleasant experiences I had during my time in Leinster House was going over when the Dáil wasn't sitting and meeting the political correspondents. Great men. Men of great integrity. Paddy Quinn, later Arthur Noonan, Michael McInerney and, probably the most objective of them all, Michael Mills and, indeed, I was not surprised when later he was selected to be the first Ombudsman of this country. His success there needs no re-telling.

Also present, as a general rule, were Jim Gibbons and Sean Dunne. Jim Gibbons was a great cartoonist and a great mimic and an even greater raconteur. He was a friendly man and a man on whose word one could always rely.

Sean Dunne was a somewhat different but even more colourful character. We were discussing one day the cost of the robes of the members of Dublin Corporation and he said: 'I don't know what the Lord Mayor's cost, but I can tell you the average one costs £84.00 and I can tell you more,' he said, 'there is no provision for them in the Laws of Lombardy.' He had obviously failed to pawn it.

Sean Dunne came to me one day and told me that he had the Leaving Cert and no Latin and, as he understood it, it was required, if he wanted to read for the Bar. He was always anxious to read for the Bar. So I told him the best thing he could do was write to the under Treasurer of King's Inns and he would get from him the time-table and the syllabus of the Latin exam and it would cost him £5.00. I didn't mention that I was the Examiner of Latin in King's Inns at the time, because I knew Sean Dunne knew that I was and, what's more, he knew that I knew that he was also aware of the same thing. He turned up to the exam and he said to me: 'I don't know much Latin.'

I said: 'I will give you the exam paper and answer book and write me an essay.'

'In Latin?' he enquired.

'Well,' I said, 'not necessarily.' You can write it in English, or any language in which you feel free to do so.' I added that he must stay for one hour.

When I took up the exam paper, the essay which I read with great interest was headed, 'The origins and growth of Irish Republicanism'. The essay ran somewhat as follows: 'Sir Robert Peel was the founder of the Republic. He set up a police force called the R.I.C. All members had to be of good physique, good looks and men that would have standing in their community. Which they had. All of these men were stationed in different numbers in different places, cities, towns, villages all over the country and being, as I have described them, they attracted the attention of the better-looking women and the better-off women. Small fellows got jealous and started shooting at them. Thus began Irish Republicanism.' He passed the exam but, for some reason known only to himself, he never started at the Bar.

He died very untimely after the 1965 General Election. He was a great speaker and began most of his speeches: 'When I was a guest of the Fianna Fáil Government in the glass-house in the Curragh' referring, of course, to his being interned during the war.

* * * *

When the 1965 election came up I was between two minds as to what I was going to do. My wife, Moya was against me running again as indeed were my family and the thought of the long weekend journeys did not inspire me either. In any event shortly before the election I was summoned by James Dillon one day to his office and he said: 'Pat, there is an election coming up and I want to read you a letter written by our election agent in Ballina saying that he has our Deputy Miko Browne standing beside him while he is dictating it and that would you like to read it?' I read it, and the gist of it was that the

Deputy in question said that his health wasn't as good as he would like it to be and accordingly his business was suffering and that going to Dublin every week didn't suit him, but that he would still stand if Pat Lindsay didn't stand, but if Pat Lindsay expressed a wish to stand he would hand him over a safe seat. So, I handed the letter back to my Leader. He said: 'Well?' and I said: 'James do you believe that?'
'Oh,' he says, 'here is a reputable election agent with one of my Deputies standing beside him telling me so – I must believe it.'
'Well,' I said 'it's not analogous, but I suppose Profumo put MacMillan into the same position'.
'Well,' says James, 'will you stand in North Mayo again in the next election?'
'James, I wouldn't touch it with a forty-foot pole'.
'Well, that's settled'.
'Well,' I said, 'with one slight addition, that you needn't believe that either.'
'My God, what it is to be the Leader of a Party.'

But he did write back and said that I had told him that I had no interest in standing, whereupon our sitting Deputy selected himself. A small group elected Tommy O'Hara who was in the wilderness at that time, he had run as an Independent in 1961, and they were looking for a non-entity in the Belmullet area where I had run for so long. All this was relayed back to me in Dublin as it was happening.

On the day of the selection convention, and unknown to Moya, I went to the house of a friend and rang the public house in Belmullet in which the convention was being held. The person who answered the phone was – and this was a total coincidence – my late brother Michael, and I said: 'Are there many there?' He said: 'Packed.' I then asked him: 'Would there be as many of them working on the day of the election?'
'Oh yes, they want you, they are sorry about the last time.'

'Well,' I said, 'get me Seamus Gaughan and John Healion.' I told them that the convention would be told that I had no interest in standing and that they were looking for somebody in Belmullet. I said to them that either one of them should propose me and the other second me before this announcement is made, and tell the convention that I am standing and when a protest is made, say that you had been on the phone to me in the last ten minutes. So that's how I was selected in 1965, almost on the spur of the moment, and certainly to the displeasure of my wife and family.

I had not been involved in any political activity in North Mayo from 1961 to 1965, except for visits to my parents home and old friends like Tony Chambers and Jack McDonald in Glenamoy and my friends in Belmullet and in Ballina. Not surprisingly Joe Leneghan now running for Fianna Fáil, made much capital of my absences – he claimed I had been in 'outer space' for the past four years. Young Eamon Waters of Ballina gave me the perfect reply which I used to good effect: 'I may have been in outer space, but I'm back, in the same capsule, flying the same flag.' When we got together after the convention I said: 'Now boys, there is one seat here certain, but there are two if we stay in our respective areas, work hard and meet only at the major rallies, at fair days in Crossmolina, Ballina, Foxford, Ballycastle, Swinford and places like that.'

We kept our agreement. We stayed in our own areas and we worked hard, and the net result was that the sitting Fine Gael TD exchanged his seat with me and Tommy O'Hara, who was our third candidate, put out Joe Leneghan so that it was an election in which we had a remarkable result. Not only did we destroy the conspirators within our own party, but we made a great national contribution by winning two seats, in this the last election, that was held in the old North Mayo constituency.

I say last election because shortly afterwards Kevin Boland, no doubt reacting to the loss of a Fianna Fáil seat, came along and revised the constituencies and changed the line in such a way that my votes were divided in half. It would take an awful lot to convince me that that particular operation was not done with the specific purpose of putting me out. That didn't particularly worry me because I was a bit anxious to get out anyway.

We were barely back in the Dáil before James Dillon resigned as party leader. He felt he had given it his best shot and it was time to make way for a younger man. Liam Cosgrave was elected without contest and certainly he was, and would have been, my first choice. I was now restored to the front bench of Fine Gael where I served during all of this Dáil. My spokesmanships were Education, and Transport and Power.

My opposite number in education was Donagh O'Malley. We got on well but I opposed his closure of the small one-teacher and two-teacher, village schools. It was at this time that I made a speech pointing out that the children who walked to the local school could observe the onset of spring, the appearance of flowers, the calves and lambs in the fields, and indeed the phenomenon of frogs jumping on the road after heavy rain. Fianna Fáil, never ones to look a gift frog in the mouth, seized on the speech and used it afterwards to jeer me.

On television on one famous occasion, I was taunted by Donagh O'Malley to 'Tell us about the frogs, Pat'. However, I enjoyed it all, and believed I was right.

We also clashed on the question of Dr John Charles McQuaid. Donagh attacked him about his attitude to Trinity College. I felt the attack had been somewhat snide, and I have never forgotten the kindness Dr McQuaid showed me when I was a young and unemployed teacher. I responded that I believed that McQuaid was a man of principle and that the worst people could say about him was that he adheres to fundamentals. I reckoned that that could not be a bad thing. I thought my remark had gone unnoticed but two days later I had a very charming letter from Dr McQuaid which thanked me for,

'Your generous and courageous tribute in the Dáil.' He told me he was particularly grateful, 'in view of the recent barrage of criticism. I only hope I have the grace to stress the fundamentals until the end.'

We met on a number of occasions after that and I have to say he lived up to my expectations. I was interested to hear on a radio programme in later years that the former Provost of Trinity College, Dr McConnell agreed that Dr McQuaid had been a man of principle who stuck to his fundamental beliefs.

I have to say however, that I also liked Donagh O'Malley enormously. I liked his panache. I liked his recklessness and above all I admired his total disregard for bureaucracy and for the Cabinet to which he belonged. His death, a terrible loss to Irish public life, saddened me enormously.

Under Liam Cosgrave's leadership there were evident tensions and strains within the Fine Gael party and in particular, within the front bench. In some ways it has been a characteristic in Fine Gael that as soon as the party gets a new leader a certain section of the party begins to look at ways and means of getting rid of him. That was certainly true, to my mind, of the advent of Liam Cosgrave to the leadership in 1965. Liam Cosgrave was a quiet man but inside him was a ring of steel that never showed itself fully. At front bench meetings I began to notice a certain linguistic interplay among three or four of its members. It was probably due to my country instinct that I came to the conclusion that a plot of some kind was underway. I should say here, that on my days on the Standing Committee of Fine Gael I had noted an antipathy on the part of old Dr Tom O'Higgins to Liam Cosgrave – ostensibly because Liam Cosgrave was reputedly 'too friendly with Sean Lemass.' I am not aware whether or not this was reciprocated by Liam Cosgrave. But I doubt it.

My doubts centered around Garret Fitzgerald, Tom O'Higgins and Declan Costello and I have to say that I also had some doubts about Gerry l'Estrange – though I am now satisfied that I was wrong there.

That doubt about Gerry l'Estrange emanated from the fact that one night at a Standing Committee meeting in Hume Street I challenged l'Estrange as to his loyalty to the leader, Liam Cosgrave. His reply was disconcerting: 'I shall always be loyal to whomsoever is leader of this party.' That satisfied me that there was a successor lurking in the wings.

Subsequently, at a front bench meeting Tom O'Higgins made a proposal that an economic advisor be appointed to the party and that he knew of one such person available. He further said that this person was prepared to resign his seat in the Dáil and take on the job full-time. He named him as none other than the then deputy for Dublin North West, Declan Costello, who happened to be absent on that day. That proposal did not have any seconder and very quickly Mark Clinton rose and spoke vehemently against it. I had had no previous discussion with Mark, but for two reasons I rose immediately to support him – firstly I had been involved in the tedious and indeed boring discussions prior to the publication of that traumatic amalgamation called *The Just Society* and secondly, I admired Mark's judgement. He was sound, sincere and convincing in argument. My main reason however was my conviction that this was the first, and as it transpired, clumsy move in a conspiracy to oust Liam Cosgrave. It was never clear who would be the leader if the plan succeeded, but I was determined to nip it in the bud. And nipped it was.

The matter went no further and Liam continued undisturbed until 1973 when he became Taoiseach.

Following his victory, the generosity of Liam Cosgrave became very apparent. He promoted the interests of all who would have chosen to oust him a year before, just prior to the Dublin bombs, when his nerve saved the day.

At this stage it may be asked why I was opposed to *The Just Society*. I have always regarded myself as a radical and have always taken the side of the small man but I felt that *The Just Society* as it was originally proposed was dangerous and unrealistic; borrowing from a number of failed systems abroad. The final *Just Society* document was a compromise and was greatly improved, indeed made respectable in the process. But my opposition also came from the fact that I was a conservative small holder from the west of Ireland. I had come up through the system and the *Just Society* in its original form contained proposals that would have outraged even the most radical members of rural and traditional Ireland.

* * * *

Then came the 1969 General Election. I didn't stand in North Mayo. I had been, as I had mentioned, 'Bolandised' and I felt there was little point in me standing now in what was virtually a new area.

Instead I stood, almost at the last minute, in Dublin North Central. I was narrowly defeated and that is something for which I am extremely grateful to the whole electorate. Bad as I was as a rural Deputy, I would have been a hopeless failure as a city representative. After that it was the law full-time for me. My practice quadrupled in that first year that I was free of politics because solicitors now knew that they would get my undivided attention.

That however was not the end of politics for me. I still remained very active in Fine Gael and was personally very close to Liam Cosgrave. I did contest Dublin North Central once again in 1973. Not surprisingly, and at no great cost to myself, I was not elected.

After becoming Master of the High Court I was constitutionally outside the political arena, but my last political act was fittingly and appropriately in my home county of Mayo, in 1975 – 38 years after I had first run for the Dáil in the old North Mayo constituency. It was to attend the convention which followed the death of one of my great friends, the late Henry Kenny. Henry, a warm kindly man whose embrace of friendship would put a ribcage at risk, and a brilliant footballer on a great Mayo team, had died with great courage and with style – now we were gathered in Castlebar to select a successor. Even though it was not wise on my part, and I felt Liam Cosgrave was not too pleased with me, I insisted on making my last political speech in the same county as I had first stood as a candidate.

To my great delight Henry's son Enda was selected, and to my even greater delight he won the by-election. My new-found judicial status did not prevent me from sharing the joy of that wonderful occasion.

Afterthoughts

As I said at the outset, this book is drawn from memory without the aid of a diary or notes. As I sit watching the now placid waters of Greatman's Bay other memories come flooding in. Many will not believe this, but my first thought is of the gong in my little church at home in Geesala.

In the course of the General Election campaign of 1954 the local curate, Fr Joe Harte, asked me, if I were to be elected, would I present a gong to the church? In view of previous experiences, the hope of election was dim, so I promised. Having been elected, Fr Harte confronted me with my promise – to which I readily acceded. It is now a happy memory to know that in my home village, my friends and neighbours are summoned by my bell to worship or to mourn.

Great characters loom into view. I think of the late Liam O'Hora, our film censor of the past, who could command attention when he began a story by saying: 'I mind the time when I was a customs officer at the Dead Sea.' It sounds extravagant but it wasn't, because he did fill such a position after leaving the Palestine police. Incidentally, the same Liam O'Hora was a member of the Irish Bar and was badly treated by the Bar Council of the day. At the time he was assistant manager of the Gaiety and it would appear to the perverse standards of the members of the Bar Council that such an occupation was in conflict with the dignity of the Bar. If poor Liam O'Hora could come back now and see and hear what's happening he would be amazed and not a little amused.

In my time in the Dáil there was a wonderful man representing South Tipperary. He was one of the two Fine Gael TDs there and his name was Pat Crowe. Now Pat Crowe was extremely popular in his own right, and he didn't have to do any of the things that most TDs and Senators do by way of letter-writing, holding clinics and all of that kind of political shennanigans which have crept into modern life. Pat Crowe avoided public meetings and he was particularly anxious to avoid becoming involved in any by-election where the whole force of the parties were thrown in. One time, however, in a Cork constituency which included Dripsey, he was forced to go. Now it should be known that Pat Crowe wrote only one letter a day while in the Dáil and that was to his wife, to whom he always affectionately referred as 'Mary O'Keeffe'. When he arrived in Dripsey he was given a wonderful introduction by the local chairman of the Fine Gael party. The candidate spoke, others spoke and finally Deputy Pat Crowe was called upon to speak. He began as follows: 'People of Dripsey I am no speaker, but if there's any place I would like to speak, it is here in Dripsey, because it is from this village that the blankets came, under which Mary O'Keeffe and I, spent many a happy night.' He stepped down off the platform, cheered to the echoes.

I recall one night in a western seaside town. It was after-hours as far as the licensing laws were concerned, but six of us were ensconced in a quiet snug in a local bar. For some reason or other, quite unexplained, the conversation of the other five turned to public schools and they worked through all of the principal public schools in England and never referred once to an Irish public school. I looked on in silence and quiet amusement because I knew that with all their inherited wealth there wasn't among the five, the makings of one Leaving Certificate or Matriculation. One of them suddenly turned to me and said: 'By the way, Pat, where were you at school?' I said: 'I am a Latinist from Killala.' The conversation ceased and there was no further reference to schools or seats of learning.

In the 1940s in Dublin I came across an extraordinary character, Dr Willie Lippman. He had seen considerable service in the East as a medical officer with the British army. When he returned to England he bought a public house in Chelsea which he used as a surgery but kept the licence going. One day as he was walking, he saw his old commanding officer approach and Willie wondered, as he said himself, whether he should speak to him or not, or whether in fact the commanding officer would know him. However, as they neared each other, Willie decided to address him and said: 'Good morning, sir, I suppose you don't remember me?' The old commanding officer adjusted his monacle, fixed him with a straight gaze and said: 'How could I ever forget that you shook the port in Kuala Lumpur.' Post-colonials and port-lovers including my friend, Colm McKeown, will understand.

My mind wanders to the banks of the Lee. I think of Denis Murphy who, like his fellow Corkmen, Jack Lynch and Stephen Barrett has helped many a lame dog over difficult stiles. I think too of the huge unemployment, not alone in Cork, but all over the country and Bill Hosford comes to mind. He told me once that a man in Kerry said to him: 'One doesn't hear anybody whistling going to work any more'; and then I can't forget my friend, John Lennon, a distinguished engineer who is successfully implementing the principles of Section 60 of the Civil Liability Act which I had caused to be inserted in that particular provision, but which no Minister has since put into force.

I think too of Brian Lenihan, a man few could dislike. I think of him with the appropriate degree of sadness by reason of the fact that the highest political price that anyone could pay was paid by him, and all in the cause of misplaced loyalty. Hard on the heels of such a thought must come Mr Charles Haughey. Charlie came into the Dáil in 1957 and it was immediately recognisable that here was a different kind of man, a man with great ability. In fact I recall at the time of his serious motor accident, somewhere in the neighbourhood of Gorey, his absence from the Dáil caused me, at any rate, to note an intellectual void in the Fianna Fáil front bench. He is without doubt, or has been up to recently, a great survivor. As an orator he was good, as a parliamentarian, more than accomplished even though some would regret that he appeared to prefer the sophists to Socrates.

Then my thoughts turn to those to whom I owe a great deal. I remember for example 1955. My correspondence was piling up relentlessly. Every new TD was plied with all the hopeless cases down the years and I found myself unable to cope, as I always did in longhand, with my correspondence. One day I went into Fine Gael headquarters seeking help and the late Maud Harding introduced me to a girl of twenty. Her name was Betty Collins and she came from Ballyheigue in Co. Kerry – Ballyheigue with its beautiful strand continuing on to Banna of Casement fame. Betty took over the job and really put in a magnificent effort. In three weeks she had cleared the whole backlog. It was Betty who taught me the meaning of the advertisers' insertions in papers when they seek 'secretarial help capable of working on her own initiative'. She removed pyramids for pittances. Later she went off to Paris, married a Frenchman and still lives there.

During the sittings of the Television Commission, I met another wonderful girl. Her name was Una McNellis from Killybegs in Donegal. She was then private secretary to Captain Drury of the Shelbourne Hotel. She took over my work in addition to whatever work she was doing for the French consortium who were interested in the television franchise. She, too, was wonderful. I think her expertise was due entirely to the fact that she hadn't attended a secondary school by reason of illness, but was ably and privately educated by her father who was the principal teacher of Killybegs national school. She married a German and is now living in Teelin in West Donegal where she runs a magnificent pub called 'The Rusty Mackerel'.

But when I no longer had the services of these two excellent girls, I was lucky to find a third who stayed with me until the end of my political life in 1969 and that was Sheila Kane, now Sheila Keenan of the Fine Gael staff.

Rightly, or wrongly, I have always equated the banking system with the usurers that Christ put out of the Temple. I did have a reputation, as Master of the High Court, of being rather severe on them. But my severity, if it was that – I would rather call it justice and equity – was brought about by the fact that I preferred to see that the rights of the small man or woman were protected. In the case of term loans, I did notice as Master of the High Court that the amount claimed included not alone payments in arrears, but that interest was added on the residue of every such payment. I asked counsel one day to get me an affidavit that the negotiating officer of the particular bank, when dealing with this client whom they were now suing had, in fact, informed him that interest would be added. For eight and half years, I never received such an affidavit and, accordingly, refused to give them compound interest. I am objecting only to the system and the system is not without its quota of greed and even in the times in which we live, the speculators are sometimes regarded as dim, shadowy figures whereas, in fact, they are the banks. Now in spite of all that, I have worked through the system and met extremely decent men whose decency wasn't in the slightest impaired by the nefarious system they were compelled to work.

Recently I met the new Provost of Trinity, Dr Thomas Mitchell, and that meeting brought my mind back to a particular area of ground outside Castlebar and made me think of the wonderful people that small area produced. Firstly the Moores of Moore Hall. John Moore was President of Connaught in 1798. Later relatives became famous writers. Then we had the Fitzgerald-Kennys, one of whom I have already referred to as 'one of my mentors'. Then came the Blowick family. Joe, of course, is well remembered as Minister for Lands and I have already referred to him. His two brothers, both priests, founded the Maynooth Mission to China and now we have Dr Thomas Mitchell from Belcarra, the Provost of Trinity and, I am proud to record, a graduate of UCG.

Any account of my life must include the name of my good and caring friend, Dr Geraldine Barniville. At some future date she will probably, in a suitable plaque, adorn a boxing stadium with a cherub at either end in the shape of Michael Carruth and Wayne McCullough; she played no mean part in their winning gold and silver medals in Barcelona.

I hope I shall be forgiven for stating how proud I am of every member of my family and how lucky I am in the spouses they selected. As I write, another grandson has been born to my younger daughter, Erris. My family have been extremely good to me, very patient, very helpful, very hospitable. I can visit them at any time without notice and be made welcome. Deep down I think they have one great regret and that is, that they weren't born before me, to bring me up properly.

I take pride in the achievements of my children and their spouses, and I delight in the company of my grandchildren. Meanwhile I continue to luxuriate in the kindness and help of my good neighbours from Casla to Lettermullen.

Epilogue

This book was launched in the Berkeley Court Hotel on 18 November, 1992. Many who wanted to be there could not for the simple reason that a General Election was in progress and politicians, who would otherwise have been present, were busy in their constituencies. But even with that there was an overflow attendance from all areas of Pat's life – lawyers, judges, academics, including the Provost of Trinity and the President of University College Dublin, politicians including former Taoiseach, Jack Lynch, journalists, family, but most of all old friends none of whom was more welcome than Pat's old hatchet man, Tony Chambers. Liam Cosgrave did the launching, touching especially on Pat's great loyalty, his humour and his love of politics.

Pat had a new suit for the occasion. There was nothing unusual in that except that he cherised the story which accompanied the buying of the suit. He was in Anthony Ryan's in Galway being advised – or bossed – by one of his committee of female organisers, when the sardonic voice of a man who had been quietly following the proceedings cut in:

'Ah Pat, I see you're chancing another one!'

The newspapers liked the book. Renagh Holohan of the *Irish Times* headed her review 'Unrepentant Blueshirt' which Pat greatly liked and described *Memories* as 'a good and enlightening read about a period few of us know much about. You can tell he had fun and we can laugh with him.' His great political opponent, Brian Lenihan, writing in the *Sunday Tribune* :

'Vitality is the pervasive Lindsay characteristic – sharp of mind and body, incisive in spirit and wit, with a mordant humour encompassed by great compassion .... wonderful company and interpreter of the human scene.' Lenihan linked him with William Norton, Leader of the Labour Party 'as the best platform speakers I have ever heard'. Lenihan recalled the fair day meeting at Ballygar mentioned by Pat in the book:

'The meeting went on half the day with Donnellan, Lindsay and Jim Hession for the Inter-party Government followed by Mark Killilea's father and the late Michael Kitt, with myself very much an acolyte in those days speaking on behalf of Fianna Fáil. Stampeding cattle and raucous hecklers from pub doorways added to the noise and gaiety of a colourful occasion'. Brian Lenihan also added that 'Lindsay was remarkably accurate and astute in his observation of people and situations, and makes his judgements without malice and with the subtlety of diminuendo. For instance he gives a high rating to Seán Lemass and Liam Cosgrave as Taoisigh, the late Niall McCarthy as a judge and Gerard Sweetman, Donogh O'Malley and Seán Dunne as politicians with flair and ability. I concur in all respects.'

In a very perceptive review in the *Irish Independent* the author and lawyer, Charles Lysaght made one point which many had missed:

'A few enemies take the rap, but the worst of them, like the prim Fine Gael barristers and the mongrel foxes are ignored, not I suspect out of kindness but because it may annoy them more!'

I can confirm that such indeed was Pat's intention. Lysaght continued, of the book:

'Bestriding the stage is Lindsay himself, a spacious, slightly irresponsible character, dedicated ultimately not to politics or the law but to laughter and the love of friends. His joy in life was refreshing ... he stood by his friends, right or wrong, especially in adversity and had it in for their enemies as well as his own. He was quick to ask a favour of a friend and equally ready to do one. Loyalty was all.'

There then followed a series of launches and book signings around the country. Galway, Cork, Ballina and Sligo and at all of them big and friendly crowds. The book stayed firmly in the bestseller chart all the way up to Christmas.

It was at this stage however that his friends and family became aware of his illness. There was little early indication that all was not well. True, his eyesight had been failing and the legs were a bit wobbly but the spirit, the curiosity and zest for life were as they had always been. But as test followed test the news was less and less good. Old friends rallied round and two in particular, Archbishop Joe Cassidy of Tuam and Liam Cosgrave gave him particular pleasure and comfort.

Pat himself knew his situation was serious. Ever a realist he was not going to fool himself but he determined to fight on. He was not afraid of death but neither was he in any great hurry. He was clear, however, that he didn't want to prolong life just for its own sake, only if he could enjoy it with dignity.

From this point onwards however the decline was rapid – but only physically because mentally he was as alert as ever, anxious for news and gossip and stories and most of all determined to be as much as possible with those he loved. His family, always the centre of his life, rallied round magnificently. It was no longer possible for him to stay on his own at Annaghvan so he alternated between Erris and Tom at Birr, Alison and Kevin in Cork and John and Fiona in Rathgar. He had time to spend with his grandchildren, something which gave him great pleasure. He had always been easy in the presence of children. He took them seriously, listened and was curious and was never too busy. It was characteristic that one of his worries as his health worsened was that he might in some way be short or irascible with any of them. He never was.

There were stays in and out of hospital. There was no hope of arresting the illness but mercifully neither was there great pain. An incident in Mount Carmel Hospital – for which hospital he had the highest praise – summed up his attitude and spirit.

He had been given some pills and given instructions as to when he could take them. He was intrigued however by the fact that each evening the nurse came and took them away. He asked her why. She was clearly a little embarrassed by the question. Pat immediately saw the humour.

'You mean, you're afraid I might take an overdose during the night?'

'Well yes' was the embarrassed reply, 'we do have to be very careful'.

'Girleen, that's one worry you needn't have about me. I intend to squeeze every last drop out of this life.'

And he meant it.

There were many farewell parties. No one called them that – except for Pat himself. Frank Conroy gave a magnificent lunch for close friends at the Berkeley Court – and it was Pat who dubbed it the 'last supper'. Every occasion was a last experience, to be enjoyed to the full. Perhaps nothing gave him greater pleasure than an invitation to lunch from Liam Cosgrave. He was touched by Liam's concern and by his thoughtfulness and that lunch at the Davenport stretched into the afternoon as they covered old ground, taking few hostages in the process but savouring every moment.

I have written in the *Sunday Tribune* of my own last two meetings with Pat. The first was at a party in my own house on 11 June – the wettest and darkest June day we've had in decades:

'Pat was dying. He knew it and we all knew it – it was obvious from his pallor and frailty. Late in the evening Pat was called upon to speak and suddenly he was transformed. The stick discarded, the cigar in one hand, a Black Bush in the other he held his audience enthralled for the next fifteen minutes.

'It was the old Pat – witty, profound, insulting to his friends but with affection and mischief, stories of North Mayo, Connemara, of old friends, old times. It was an astonishing performance. When he sat down he was drained but he knew – as we did – that this was his 'last hurrah', and by sheer willpower he ensured it would live forever in the memories of those who were there. As it will.

'My last meeting with Pat was three weeks ago this Sunday. It was in Dessie Hynes' pub in Rathmines and once again he was in his element. Stories, memories, old battles, old scores, both settled and still to be settled. It went on and on, while I became more and more concerned about the toll this was taking on his stamina, until suddenly it dawned on me that Pat intended to die as he had lived – squeezing every last drop of enjoyment out of life to the very end. Every experience was to be savoured to the full. Life was there to be celebrated. And celebrate it he did.'

Pat made his last journey westward on 17 June, travelling with his great and generous friend, Dessie Hynes. It was clear he wanted to die in Annaghvan in his beloved Connemara and his journey back was a last look at scenes and places that had been so much part of his life. There was a nostalgic stop at Furey's of Moyvalley and another at Cawley's of Craughwell and after a short break with Alison at Nun's Island in Galway it was off to Annaghvan. Once again family and close friends enriched his last days and it was in the presence of Fiona whom he so greatly liked and admired that the end came, peacefully and calmly on Tuesday 29 June.

That afternoon both Dáil and Seanad interrupted business to pay tribute. The Taoiseach, Albert Reynolds, referred to him as 'a skilled parliamentarian and advocate'. John Bruton in a warm and eloquent speech covered many aspects of his life, referring in particular to 'the enormous strength of his personal character ... and his unique combination of legal knowledge and earthy common sense.' All parties joined in both Houses in paying tribute.

Pat was buried at Deansgrange Cemetery on 1 July beside his beloved Moya. The funeral was as he would have liked it. The President of Ireland honoured his memory with her presence. His friend, Joe Cassidy, said the mass and delivered the homily. Liam Cosgrave spoke over the grave. And his grandchildren carried the offerings at mass – his cigars, his unfinished crossword, the last of the Black Bush.

I wrote of Pat the following Sunday in the *Sunday Tribune* :

'Pat Lindsay is most often referred to as a great story teller, a wonderful raconteur. And he was. The commanding physical presence, the wonderfully resonant voice, the bushy eyebrows, the ever-present cigar, the natural acting talents. But as his old friend, Archbishop Joseph Cassidy, said in his moving tribute at Thursday's mass, there was far more to it than that.

'There was real substance underpinning the stories, a substance born out of a myriad experiences, growing up in North Mayo, the student days in Galway, the rakish years as an impoverished but resourceful teacher, the decades in politics and the law. Most of all there was his unquenchable curiosity about his fellow men – and women – because Pat was also a great listener, a great observer of human nature in all its manifestations and a great, if sometimes obstinate, judge of human nature.

'Pat was above all else a people person. He was the opposite of so many of our trendy socialists who bleed for humanity but ignore the individual. For him the person was everything – and especially the small person, the weak and defenceless.

'As master of the High Court he had a chance to put his philosophy into practice. He believed that big institutions, the banks, insurance companies, the Revenue and big business had the resources to hire the best legal talent available. The small person, the individual, was often on his own, so Pat evened up the balance by doing everything in his power to frustrate the big players – something he did with relish and even a little malice and to the great annoyance of those institutions.

'Pat was not a particularly successful politician. He was out of the Dáil as often as he was in and his ministerial career was cut short by the inter-party defeat in 1957 and by the fact that his party was in continuous opposition for 16 years when Pat was in his prime and would have held high office.

'It's impossible to say what sort of minister he would have been. Most likely he would have been in the mould of his great friend, Donogh O'Malley – irreverent, rumbustious, unpredictable but certainly creative. One thing is certain – he would not have been a civil servants' minister.

'For him in politics, loyalty was the greatest of all values. His belief in Fine Gael, and especially in the party's core values, was total. He was particularly loyal to its leaders.

'With James Dillon he had a great deal in common, a shared love of the West of Ireland, of the small farm, of the settled traditional values. With Liam Cosgrave he had one of his closest and most enduring friendships, and Liam Cosgrave never had a stronger supporter or defender than Pat Lindsay. He would have enjoyed Liam's valedictory words at the graveside last Thursday.

'It has to be said that he was not comfortable with the Just Society, partly because he distrusted its authors and partly because he felt it was unrealistic and borrowed from failed overseas systems. But whether he agreed or disagreed, his public support for the party and his defence of it never wavered.

'Friendship and fun were two of his greatest characteristics. He could be devastatingly insulting to those he found pretentious or false, and his mind, once made up about somebody, was not easily changed. As an enemy he did not take hostages, but on the other hand friendship was total.

'At a time when there was little inter-party socialising in Leinster House Pat made lifelong friends in Fianna Fáil. He was fascinated by some of the more unorthodox Fianna Fáil backbenchers like the 'Fiddler' Flynn from Kerry or John Moher from Cork; he had great admiration for Sean Lemass and enjoyed the company of Sean MacEntee and Brian Lenihan. But for the boring or the pompous, in his own party or others, there was no time whatsoever.

'There is so much more one could write about Pat Lindsay. He lived life more than to the full. At times he was reckless, at times excessive and he would want me to say so. But his faults were minuscule compared to his virtues.

'Above all else was his sheer gargantuan humanity which permeated everything he did and made knowing him an unforgettable experience and sharing his friendship a privilege beyond compare.'

And in the course of a warm tribute in the *Sunday Press,* John Boland has his memory of Pat and the funeral.

'You only know the value of loyalty when you discover that you have not got it.

'The gravelly voice was unmistakable, the message, as it always was, clear and crisp. Just occasionally, last Thursday, one felt as if we were in a time warp, participating in archive footage from the Seventies. Despite the brilliant sunshine, if everything had turned black and white we would have understood.

'The little man spoke with authority, with certainty of belief, and, as always, with his native Dublin wit and humour. Liam Cosgrave was paying his last respects at the graveside of his friend and political colleague, Pat Lindsay.

'... For a few hours on Wednesday evening, and again in the South Dublin summer morning on Thursday, one remembered, and understood, what Fine Gael stood for. You did not have to be of that stock to hear the message – Pat Lindsay's church was broad and his funeral attendance spanned many beliefs.'

Brian Lenihan heard the message and knew who it was meant for.

'Not for us, he smiled later, but your former colleagues should have listened carefully!' How right he was. Brian is a good politician and has always had the capacity to admire another. That is why he was at Lindsay's funeral – and why he spent so long chatting with Liam Cosgrave afterwards.

'... Lindsay, for example, would have given his last shilling to buy a meal for a hungry colleague. During his funeral mass, Tony Chambers, the orchestra leader made famous by the "Ballroom of Romance", blew "Amazing Grace" on the saxophone. Probably the first time he had played toffee-nosed Mount Merrion. No sopranos nor Missa Cantatas for Pat Lindsay. He had walked with kings yet had not lost the common touch.

'And if some of the congregation who fancy themselves as kings or queens were slightly bemused, then Lindsay would have been delighted. His friend – his loyal friend – was paying the final tribute.

'Tony told us that he had first worked for Paddy in the 1937 election. Over fifty years ago. How many of the present crop can expect such loyalty from their workers?

'And how many deserve it?'

However let's leave the last word with Pat himself. In June, despite his ill health, he had recorded an interview with John Quinn for the RTE programme *My Education*. The interview was broadcast after his death and he knew it would be his last public word. He ended on this note:

'I enjoyed everything ... even the forbidden things ... maybe especially the forbidden things ... I loved every bit of it ... a fellow asked me maybe a year or two ago what my greatest achievement in life was. The greatest achievement that anybody can have in life is the making of good and sincere friends and holding them.'

Senator Maurice Manning
October 1993

Index